11/75

With lots of love from

Uncle Trevor &

Auntie Pat

Christmas 1979.

To

SARAH JANE

Eckett

THE RUTH AINSWORTH BOOK

Books by

RUTH AINSWORTH

Fiction

Fairy Gold
Jack Frost
Listen With Mother Tales
Look, Do and Listen
Roly the Railway Mouse
Rufty Tufty Flies High
Rufty Tufty Goes Camping
Rufty Tufty the Golliwog
Rufty Tufty and Hattie
Rufty Tufty's Island
Rufty Tufty Runs Away
Rufty Tufty at the Seaside
Rufty Tufty Makes a House
The Wolf Who Was Sorry

Non-Fiction

Look About You Books

1. *In Woods and Fields*
2. *Down the Lane*
3. *Beside the Sea*
4. *By Pond and Stream*
5. *In the Park*
6. *In Your Garden*

Ruth Ainsworth

THE RUTH AINSWORTH BOOK

Illustrated by
SHIRLEY HUGHES

HEINEMANN : LONDON

William Heinemann Limited
15 Queen Street, Mayfair, London WIX 8 BE
LONDON MELBOURNE TORONTO
JOHANNESBURG AUCKLAND

First published 1970
Reprinted 1974

434 92584 5

Printed and bound in Austria
by Wiener Verlag, Vienna

Contents

Charles and the Pine-cones

There was once a little boy called Charles who liked collecting things. Sometimes he collected acorns. Sometimes he collected chestnuts. Sometimes he collected bus tickets. His pockets were always very full of whatever he was collecting at the time. His mother gave him a big brown-paper bag to put his things in, but the bag soon broke because he filled it too full.

One day, Charles' grandmother made him a bright blue bag with a piece of tape threaded through the top, so he could draw the tape tight and close the bag safely. It was a large, strong bag. She sewed some words on the bag in white braid and the words read: MY USEFUL BAG.

Charles loved his Useful Bag. It was nearly as big as a sack. Just then he was collecting pine-cones and every afternoon his mother took him into a little wood, where pine trees grew. There were lots of pine-cones lying on the ground and Charles picked up all he could see and put them into his bright blue bag.

"What will you do with all those pine-cones?" asked his mother.

"What will you do with all those pine-cones?" asked his father.

"What will you do with all those pine-cones?" asked the milkman and the postman and the baker.

"I don't know," said Charles, "but they will come in useful one day." And he went on picking up pine-cones and dropping them into his bright blue bag. Soon the bag was nearly full.

One afternoon, Charles was going to the woods with his mother when he saw an old man sitting by a hedge. The old man had made a little fire and he was holding a frying-pan over the fire, cooking some bacon in it. The fire looked as if it would go out any minute. There were no flames, only a curl of gray smoke.

"Why doesn't your bacon spit and sizzle like our bacon does at home?" asked Charles.

"Because my fire is so small," said the old man. "If I had a big, hot, fire, my bacon would spit and sizzle like yours."

"I will make your fire hot," said Charles, and he undid the tape round the mouth of his bag and tipped out all his pine-cones.

The old man put the pine-cones on the fire; first a small handful, then a bigger handful, then more and more till the fire burned bright and the bacon spat and sizzled.

"Thank you very much," said the old man. "Now my bacon will taste crisp and good. I have something in my pocket I should like to give you."

He put his hand into his pocket and brought out a little wooden boat. It had two masts and a rudder.

"I made this myself with my knife," he said. "You can sail it in your bath."

Charles thanked the old man very much and that night he sailed the wooden boat in his bath. It sailed very well. He made little waves with his hands and even then it did not upset. It was the best boat he had ever had.

What the Kitten Caught

There was once a little girl called Jane who had a kitten called Smuts. Smuts was a clever little black kitten, who liked catching things. Especially things that moved. He jumped after leaves as they blew about the garden. He jumped after flies. He jumped after bits of string that Jane pulled along the floor. He turned round and round and round, chasing the tip of his own black tail; round and round and round till his little black head was dizzy.

One day, Smuts came trotting in from the garden,

carrying something in his mouth. He was feeling very proud of himself. His tail stuck straight up in the air and he was purring deep down in his throat. A very pleased, contented kind of purr.

"Oh, Smuts, whatever have you caught now?" said Jane. "I hope it isn't a bird. Do let me look and see what you are carrying."

But Smuts crouched down on the rug and would not let Jane look.

Then the thing in his mouth gave a sharp little squeak, like this—Squeak! Squeak! Squeak!

"Oh dear!" said Jane. "I believe you have caught a mouse. Do, please, let it go and I will give you some fish instead."

But Smuts crouched down lower on the rug and the purr turned into a growl, like this—Gr-r-r-r-r. He was so pleased with what he had caught that he could not bear to let it go.

Then the thing in his mouth squeaked again. This time the squeak did not sound like a mouse. Oh no—it sounded like someone calling out, "Help! Help! Help!"

Smuts was so surprised that he opened his mouth a little and the thing he was carrying wriggled out and scurried across the rug and got under a chair. It was a little Fairy Man, no bigger than a mouse.

Jane picked him up and looked at him. He was simply furious. His cheeks were red with anger and he was frowning. He stamped his foot and spluttered in a cross voice:

"Take that huge, horrible tiger away. It nearly ate me up!"

"Never mind," said Jane. "It is only Smuts, my kitten. He wouldn't really hurt you. Let me tidy you up a little and you'll feel better."

She brushed his coat and did up a button and tidied his hair. But he was still very cross.

"My afternoon is spoiled," he said. "I was going out to tea with my best friend and we were going to have strawberry jam and iced cake. Now I can't go. It's a shame."

"Why can't you go?" asked Jane, wiping his face with the corner of her handkerchief. "You look quite tidy and nice now."

"Don't ask silly questions," went on the Fairy Man. "Of course I can't go. I've lost my hat, for one thing, and I've dropped my present. It is my friend's birthday and I was taking him a dandelion clock. Oh dear, I *am* disappointed."

"Don't be so sad," said Jane. "I'll find you a new hat and another present. Wait while I get them."

She ran out into the garden and came back with an

acorn cup and a dandelion clock. The acorn cup just fitted on the Fairy Man's head and he was very pleased with the dandelion clock.

"Does the hat really suit me?" he asked.

"Oh yes," said Jane, and she held him up and let him see himself in the looking-glass. He turned his head this way and that. Yes, the hat really suited him. It fitted just as if it had been made for him.

"My friend lives in the beech tree," said the Fairy Man. "If you can take me there, I shall be just in time. I must be there before they start the strawberry jam and the iced cake."

So Jane carried him outside and put him down at the foot of the beech tree and he disappeared inside a little hole among the roots. Smuts was quite happy because he found a feather to play with instead. He pounced on it and shook it and threw it up into the air. And no one tried to take it away from him.

Charles and the Braided String

Do you remember a story about a boy called Charles who was always collecting things? He collected pine-cones and kept them in the Useful Bag his grandmother had made for him. This is another story about Charles.

When Charles was tired of collecting pine-cones, he began to collect string. He saved all the string off his birthday presents and if he saw anyone undoing a parcel he always asked: "May I have that piece of string, please, if you can spare it?"

Soon he had lots of pieces of string in his Useful Bag. One day his mother helped him to join the pieces together with knots till he had three long pieces of string instead of lots and lots of short pieces.

"Will you teach me how to braid them?" he asked. So his mother taught him how to braid them. I expect you have seen little girls with their hair made into a braid, sometimes one braid and sometimes two. Perhaps, if you are a girl, you have braids yourself.

Charles' braid grew longer and longer till he had used up all the three pieces of string and made them into a string braid rather like a rope.

"What will you do with your string braid?" asked Mother.

"What will you do with your string braid?" asked Father.

"What will you do with your string braid?" asked the milkman and the postman and the baker.

"I don't know," said Charles, "but it will come in handy one day." Wherever he went he carried the string braid in his pocket.

One morning he was out shopping with Mother and suddenly a little black and white puppy ran right across the busy road. The automobiles put on their brakes—squeak! squeak! The buses blew their horns—poop! poop!

People on bicycles rang their bells—ting-a-ling! ting-a-ling! The little black and white puppy yelped with fright—yelp! yelp!

Then a little girl ran to the puppy and took him up in her arms and stroked him and comforted him. "You must not go on to the road," she said. "You might get hurt."

"Is he your puppy?" asked Charles' mother.

"Yes," said the little girl. "I have bought him a collar but I have lost his lead. And he is so lively that he won't stay on the path and I am afraid he may get run over."

"I can give you a lead," said Charles. "A good, strong lead. Then he will be safe." He put his hand in his pocket and brought out his string braid.

"Thank you," said the little girl. "It is just what I wanted."

Charles' mother fastened one end to the puppy's collar and the little girl held the other end in her hand. They went off together, the little girl smiling and the black and white puppy frisking about on his new lead.

Charles was happy too. His string braid had come in handy after all.

Charles makes a House

Charles was very fond of making houses. Sometimes he made a house under the nursery table. Sometimes he put a rug over two chairs and made a house that way. Sometimes he crept inside the toy cupboard and *nearly* shut the door, leaving just a crack showing, and that made a small, dark, secret little house.

One day, when Charles was playing in the yard, he saw a hole at the foot of a tree, between two of the big roots. It was large enough to put both his hands inside. "What a nice little house that hole would make," he thought. "Not for me, of course, but for somebody very small."

He found some moss under the ferns nearby and made a green, mossy carpet for the floor. Then he picked a toadstool and stood it in the middle for a table. He scattered rose petals on the carpet to look pretty and smell nice.

Charles had a sand-box in another part of the garden and he took some sand in his seaside pail to make a sandy path, leading to the door. Just outside the door he put a tin lid filled with water, so that anyone living in the house could have a drink when he wanted it.

There were some other little holes between the roots of the tree and these would be fine for cupboards and shelves. In one he put a pile of twigs, broken into tiny pieces for firewood. In another he put some good things to eat like parsley and mint and a pod of peas.

When it was time to go to bed, Charles did not want to leave his little house. He lay down flat on the ground and looked right inside and he wished he were small enough to live there. The mossy floor was so green and soft and the rose petals were such a pretty pink.

The next morning, after breakfast, Charles ran down the yard to see if the house was all right. He peeped inside the door. It looked just the same, very cozy but quite, quite empty. He did wish someone was living there.

He scattered fresh petals on the floor and watered the moss with his watering-can, to keep it green and damp.

The next morning, after breakfast, Charles ran down the yard again to see if the house was all right. This time, as he peeped inside, he saw a little, shining, silvery track on the floor. Someone had crept up the sandy path and round the toadstool table, over the rose petals. It must have been a snail, because a snail always leaves a silvery track behind him.

But the snail had gone away. The little house was quite, quite empty again.

"Anyhow," thought Charles, "snails carry their houses on their backs. They don't need to live in *my* little house."

He scattered more fresh petals on the floor and watered the moss with his watering-can, to keep it green and damp.

The next morning, after breakfast, Charles ran down the yard to see if the little house was all right. He peeped inside the door and a small, brown face with very bright eyes peeped out at him. It was a frog. It gave Charles a

friendly look and then hopped slowly away. The moss and the petals were flat, so perhaps the frog had slept there all night.

Charles' mother wrote FROG HOUSE on a strip of

paper and pinned it on the tree, just above the door.

Charles was so happy that someone was living in his house. He watered the moss every day to keep it fresh, and scattered new petals on the floor. He hoped the friendly frog would often sleep there and perhaps paddle in the tin lid of water.

Charles' Long Morning

One day, Charles woke up feeling excited. In the afternoon he was going to a party at the house of his friend Jane. It was Jane's birthday. Charles talked about the party while he was getting up and having his breakfast. He *did* wish it was time to get ready and go!

"What shall I do all the morning?" he asked his mother

"Why don't you play out in the yard," she said. "The sun is shining and there are always lots of things to do outside."

So Charles went into the garden. First he bounced his ball on the path. It was a brown, rubber ball and it bounced well, but it kept rolling off the path and disappearing under the rhubarb leaves. Then he had to creep under the leaves to find it. So he soon got tired of playing with his ball.

"Is it time for the party?" he asked.

"No," said his mother. "It is only nine o'clock."

Then he got his tricycle out of the shed and rode up and down the lawn. The lawn sloped and he liked riding *down* the slope, ringing his bell. But it was hard work riding *up* the slope. It made his legs ache. So he got tired of playing with his tricycle.

"Is it time for the party?" he asked.

"No," said his mother, "it is only ten o'clock."

Then he put his teddy bear in his wheelbarrow and gave him rides round the house. Round and round and round they went. Sometimes he ran and then the wheelbarrow went bump—bump—bump—and teddy bear fell out. So he soon got tired of playing with his wheelbarrow and went indoors to find his mother.

"Is it time for the party?" he asked.

"No," said his mother, "it is only eleven o'clock."

Charles went back into the garden to the place where the foxgloves grew. They were very tall, taller than he was. Some were white and some were pink. They were nearly through blooming and many of the flowers had

dropped off on to the ground. Charles managed to find ten white flowers and he fitted them on the tops of his fingers and his two thumbs. They felt cool and soft. Then he crept into the kitchen and said to his mother, "Shut your eyes. The Foxglove Man has come to tickle you."

So she shut her eyes and he tickled her face with his white, foxglove fingers and stroked her neck and arms.

"You mustn't laugh, or the Foxglove Man will be angry!"

She tried not to laugh, though the foxglove fingers tickled terribly. Then Charles let her open her eyes and they both laughed and the foxglove fingers fell off.

"Is it time for the party?" he asked.

"No, it is only twelve o'clock," said his mother. "Why don't you take your rug and spread it in the shade and lie on it for a little while."

Charles took his rug and spread it in the shade and lay down on it. The daisies on the lawn looked quite tall when he lay down flat. A little beetle was sitting on one daisy and when the wind blew, the daisy swayed to and fro, to and fro, and gave the little beetle a ride.

A grasshopper was chirping, "Chip! Chip! Chip!"

A bird in a bush was talking to her babies, "Chirrup! Chirrup! Chirrup!"

The leaves on the trees were rustling, "Sh-wish! Sh-wish! Sh-wish!"

Charles felt very sleepy. He closed his eyes. He fell asleep. When he woke, his mother was bending over him.

"Is it time for the party?" he asked.

"It is one o'clock," she said. "When you have had your

dinner and washed yourself and put on your clean blue suit, it will be time to start."

Charles jumped up and ran indoors. The party was almost there. The long morning was over.

Charles and Jenny

"Will you come and help me to put up the camp bed in your bedroom, Charles?" said his mother. "Your cousin Jenny is coming to stay. She is four, like you."

As they spread the sheets and blankets on the little bed, Charles wondered what Jenny would be like. He had not seen her for so long that he could not remember anything about her.

"You will enjoy having someone to play with," said Mother.

"Yes," said Charles, though he did not look pleased. "She can play with my toys but she can't see what is in my USEFUL BAG. That's a secret." His blue bag was slung over one shoulder and he gave it a pat and smiled.

Only he knew what was inside.

Jenny came the next day. Charles thought she looked very nice. She had short, yellow braids, tied with red ribbons.

He showed her his toys in the cupboard and on the shelf and then she caught sight of the blue bag which he had hidden behind the box of building blocks.

"What do you keep in this big bag?" she asked and

before Charles could stop her, she had opened the mouth of it and put in her hand.

"Leave my bag alone!" shouted Charles. "It's my very own secret bag. Give it back!" and he snatched at the bag.

"I only wanted to have a LOOK!" shouted Jenny, holding fast to the string.

Just then Mother came in to say that dinner was ready. Jenny let go of the string and Charles carried the bag into the dining-room and hung it on the back of his chair, while he ate.

After dinner Mother said to them, "I have an idea for an indoor game. It's too wet to play in the yard. But I need two empty match-boxes, one each. And I can't find two anywhere. It is a pity."

Charles smiled and opened his blue bag and fumbled about inside and brought out two empty match-boxes.

"What a useful bag!" said Mother. "There's no guessing what's inside. Now this is the game. See how many tiny things you can collect in your match-box. But you must only have one of each kind. You can go where you like in the house."

Charles was still a little bit cross. "Jenny's match-box is bigger than mine," he grumbled. "It will hold more things."

"Let's measure and see," said Mother. So they laid one

match-box on top of the other and they were exactly the same size.

Then Charles and Jenny ran off to look for tiny things to put in their match-boxes. They went everywhere, upstairs and downstairs, in and out of the bedrooms, in and out of the dining-room, in and out of the kitchen. They got out of breath with running and their cheeks were red and hot. Once they bumped into each other in the hall and they both laughed.

"I've found something else," said Jenny, taking a pin off the pincushion.

"So have I," said Charles, dropping a tiny glass bead into his match-box.

It would take too long to tell you ALL the things they managed to squeeze in. When Mother called, "Time is up," the lids would barely slide on, the boxes were so full. They emptied them out on the kitchen table and Mother counted them. Jenny had twenty-five things and Charles had one less—he had twenty-four.

I will tell you some of Jenny's things: a piece of cotton, a cornflake, a feather, a button, a pin and a crumb.

Now I will tell you some of Charles' things: a match, a bead, a grain of rice, a stamp, a raisin and a hair. The hair was a curly brown one. He had pulled it out of his own head.

Charles was not at all cross now. He did not mind Jenny having one more thing than he had.

"Let's play this game again," said Charles. "Can we go out in the yard now the rain has stopped? Would you like to play it again, Jenny?"

"Yes, I would," said Jenny.

"You can play it in the garden if you wear galoshes," said Mother. So they put on their galoshes and ran outside.

There were not so many tiny things in the garden, but

they collected petals and leaves and seeds and berries. When the time was up and Mother counted, Charles had twelve things and Jenny had eleven.

After lunch, Charles opened his Useful Bag and told Jenny she could look inside if she wanted. It was half full of things to keep other things in: there were tins and little bottles and match-boxes and jars with screw lids. "We might play store with all these good things," said Jenny.

"So we will, tomorrow," said Charles. "We will ask Mother to give us some real rice and coffee and sugar to put in the jars."

Charles was glad that Jenny had come to stay a while at his house. Jenny was glad too.

Charles on a Windy Day

One morning, after breakfast, Charles' mother said to him: "I should like to wash your Useful Bag today."

"But it doesn't need washing," said Charles. "It's quite clean."

"Let's look and see," said Mother, and she spread the bag out on the table. It was very dirty indeed. There were brown marks of mud on it and green marks of wet grass, because Charles took his Useful Bag everywhere with him and he often went in dirty places.

"It is a bit dirty," agreed Charles; "but don't wash it today. Not today. Another day."

"The sun is shining and the wind is blowing," said his mother, "and the bag will be dry in a jiffy. Then I will iron it and you can have it back by dinner-time."

"Y-e-e-e-s," said Charles. "But what shall I do with the things from inside? I need a safe place to put them."

"You can have this big shopping bag with string handles. That will do just for now."

"All right," said Charles, unpacking his things from the blue bag and putting them into the shopping bag. "But my bag doesn't often need washing. Not again for another year."

Mother quickly put some soap-flakes in a bowl of water and whisked them up with her hand till the water was all foamy. Then she plunged the bag into the bowl. She squeezed and squeezed till the bag was clean, and after she rinsed it in a bowl of clear water, she wrung it as dry as she could.

"I'll put it on the clothes line," said Charles.

"Shall I help as the wind is so strong?" asked Mother.

"Please don't come. Please don't help. I can do it by myself," said Charles. So he took the wet bag into the garden and got two clothes-pins from the pin-basket in the shed. The line was low and he could reach it. He put a clothes-pin at each corner and watched the wind blow the bag till it was like a blue balloon.

Charles liked to hear the flapping noise it made—flappity—flappity—flap—flap—flap! Then he went indoors to play with his train. When he had played trains long enough, he ran outside to see if his bag was dry.

Oh, what could have happened? The line was still there, but there was nothing on it. The two clothes-pins that had held the corners of his bag were lying on the grass.

"Mother!" he called. "Mother! Come help me! The wind has blown my bag away!"

His mother came hurrying into the garden. She saw the empty line and the two clothes-pins and Charles' sad face.

"We'll find your bag," she said. "It can't be far off. Let's both look. It may be caught in a tree or bush."

The wind was very strong. It tangled their hair and snatched at the strings of Mother's apron. Up in the sky the big white clouds were scurrying along.

Charles felt sure his bag had gone whirling away, high in the air, so he looked in all the high places. He looked at the tops of the trees and the roof of the house. His neck ached because he bent it back so far. But there was nothing blue caught in the trees or on the roof or by the chimneys.

His mother looked lower down. She searched the bushes and the hedge. But there was nothing blue caught in the bushes or the hedge.

"Perhaps it is miles away," said Charles. "Miles and miles away where we shall never find it."

"Let's walk all round the garden once more," said Mother. "Then we can try the yard next door."

So they walked slowly round the garden, looking among the potatoes and the cabbages and the flowers, searching everywhere. Suddenly Charles cried out:

"Mother! Look! In the long grass behind the summer-house!"

She looked in the long grass and there was the bag. Charles ran to pick it up, but he stopped when he had touched the string.

"There's something *in* my bag," he whispered. "I saw it move. A kind of little lump."

They both watched. There was a small hump at the bottom, not much bigger than a marble.

"It moved. It's alive," said Charles.

The small hump moved a little way. Then stopped. Moved a little farther. Stopped again.

"Is it a bird?" wondered Charles, "or a snail?"

The hump moved very quickly, far too quickly for a

snail. Charles watched the mouth of the bag. Would the little thing peep out? Did it like being shut up in a bag?

Suddenly a tiny face appeared, the tiniest face Charles had ever seen. It had ears and a sharp nose and bright eyes. And tiny, tiny whiskers.

"A baby mouse!" whispered Charles. "It has a very lost look."

The baby mouse came right out of the bag so they could see its little feet and long tail. It looked one way. Then the other. Then it turned all the way around. For the mouse, the grass was a tall forest and it could only peer between the stalks.

"Will it ever find the way home?" asked Charles. "It's only a baby. Can we have it for a pet?"

But the baby mouse was very sensible though it was so small. It went on looking and sniffing and turning around and trying to remember where it lived. Then it gave a happy little scamper and darted through the grass and dived into a hole under the summer-house.

"I expect its mother is glad," said Charles. "She must take better care of it till it grows bigger."

Then they went indoors. Mother washed the bag again because it had got dirty and pinned it on the line herself with four clothes-pins to keep it safe, one at each corner and two in the middle. Charles had a glass of milk and two ginger cookies.

"Looking for lost things makes me hungry," said Charles, scrunching his hard cookies and drinking the last drop of his milk.

Charles is Cross

There was once a little boy called Charles who had a Useful Bag to keep his treasures in. Later in the story I will tell you more about the Useful Bag.

"I don't know what to do," said Charles, one damp,

dull morning. "There's nothing in the world I want to do."

"Let's try to think of something," said his mother. "The rain has stopped. Why don't you put on your galoshes and play in the garden?"

Charles' galoshes were red and he was very fond of them, but on this particular day he felt cross and contrary.

"I'll play in the garden," he said. "But not in my galoshes."

"What a pity," said his mother. "You'll have to play indoors instead as the garden is far too wet for shoes."

"I don't care," said Charles. "I like indoors best." This was not really true, but he still felt cross.

First he got out his coloring book and began to color a very nice picture of a train. He snatched up the crayons and pressed so hard that he broke a green one doing the engine. A red one doing the signal. A blue one doing the sky. A yellow one doing the sun. And a black one doing the smoke. So they were all broken.

Then he pulled his box of building blocks from under the table and began to build a tall tower. He piled the bricks just anyhow. Sometimes a large one. Then a small one. Then a wide one. Then a narrow one. The tower rocked and swayed and fell down with a crash.

The sun came out and shone through the window and

Charles could see millions of specks of dust dancing in a sunbeam. How lovely it would be in the garden. But he had said he would not wear his galoshes and he was still too cross to change his mind.

Mother brought him his orange juice and a cookie.

"I don't want any," said Charles.

"Very well," said his mother, putting away the juice and the cookie. Charles felt sorry he had not drunk his juice because he was thirsty, but he did not feel like asking to have it brought back.

"Now it is time for your rest," went on his mother.

"I won't go to sleep. I won't *ever* go to sleep."

"Never mind. You can stay awake. People can rest without going to sleep."

Still grumbling, Charles stumped upstairs, thump, thump, thump, and mother took off his shoes and tucked him under the blankets.

"I won't lie down. I'll sit up."

"Very well. You can rest sitting up." Charles sat up in his blue bathrobe, looking very wide awake.

"Here is your Useful Bag," said his mother, handing him the special bag where he kept his treasures. "I've put a surprise in it."

Every day at rest time, Charles' mother put a surprise in his Useful Bag. It was not anything new, bought at the shops. It was just one of his own toys that he had not played with lately. He always looked forward to plunging his hand deep into the bag and fumbling about till he had found the special thing.

Today, when he fumbled about, he found his monkey glove inside. It was a little, soft monkey head with two little monkey arms, shaped like a glove. He could put his hand inside and when he moved his fingers and thumb, the monkey nodded and moved his arms. Charles loved his monkey glove and he and monkey had long talks together. Of course he had to talk *for* monkey, but he used a special squeaky voice and they got on very well.

"Hello, monkey," said Charles.

"Hello, Charles," said monkey.

"Where have you been all this time?"

"I've been climbing a coconut tree to get coconuts."

"Did you find any?"

"Yes. I found a hundred. I drank the milk and ate so much nut that I got hiccoughs."

Charles felt rather sleepy, but he still sat up.

"Are you tired, monkey?"

"Yes, Charles. Very very tired."

"Then let's lie down."

Charles and monkey snuggled down together.

"Shall I say 'Peter Piper' to you, monkey?"

"Yes, please."

But before Charles could finish, he was fast asleep and he slept and slept till the cuckoo clock on the wall called "Cuckoo!" once.

That meant one o'clock and as he opened his eyes, his mother came in to wake him. He washed his hands and went downstairs with monkey to have his dinner.

"Oh, what a lovely dinner. A bird's nest," said Charles, which was his name for a poached egg sitting in a nest of mashed potatoes.

Then came a dish of ice-cream. Charles felt happy again and when he had listened to a story on the TV, he got ready for his walk.

"I'll put my galoshes on myself," said Charles cheerfully and he pulled and tugged and got them on with no help.

"Can monkey come for a walk?"

"Yes, of course he can," said Mother. So Charles wore a monkey glove on one hand and a knitted glove on the other.

As Charles splashed through the puddles, he talked to monkey.

"Wasn't I cross this morning?"

"Oh, you were cross," agreed monkey. "Cross as two sticks."

"I was as cross as TWENTY sticks. But I'm not cross now. I don't think I shall ever be cross again."

"Oh goody! goody!" squeaked monkey, nodding his little monkey head and waving his paws, to show he was happy.

Pepper and Salt

There were once two little kittens who were brothers. They were both born on the same day, so they were twin brothers. They did everything together. When one opened his eyes, the other opened his eyes too. So they *both* opened their eyes.

When one learned to lap milk out of a saucer, the other learned to lap milk out of a saucer too. So they *both* lapped milk out of a saucer.

When one began to chase his tail, the other began to chase his tail too. So they *both* chased their tails.

One kitten was all white. He was called Salt. The other was white with patches of gray fur here and there. He was called Pepper. They had a nice, kind, sleepy mother called Mrs. Tabby. They all slept together in a box under the kitchen table.

One day, Salt said to Pepper: "I can climb higher than you!"

"No, you can't!" said Pepper. "*I* can climb higher than *you*!"

"Let's find a tall tree and I'll show you," said Salt.

"Yes, let's," agreed Pepper. "And *I'll* show *you*."

They ran into the garden and found a tall fir tree. It went up—up—up—higher than the house. The little kittens began to climb. They had never climbed a tree before and they did not enjoy climbing this one. The bark was rough and slippery. The green, pointed leaves pricked their soft pink noses. But they went on and on, higher and higher. At last they reached the top.

"We are on the same branch," said Salt, "so we are as high as each other."

"So we are," said Pepper. "Now we must go down.

Mother will be wondering where we are."

But they couldn't get down. There was no room to turn round and they dared not climb backwards. They were stuck fast. The ground looked a terrible way off. If they fell, they would certainly break some bones.

A big bird flew over the tree.

"Miaow! Miaow! Miaow!" cried the kittens. "Please help us to get down."

But the big bird flew on its way, calling: "Cuckoo! Cuckoo! Cuckoo!"

Then an aeroplane dived out of the clouds above them.

"Miaow! Miaow! Miaow!" cried the kittens. "Please help us to get down!"

But the aeroplane went zooming on its way, z-z-z-z-z-z.

The sun set and the night wind blew through the garden, shaking the fir tree.

"Miaow! Miaow! Miaow!" cried the kittens. "Please blow us down to the ground."

But the night wind went whistling on its way, whoo—oo—whoo.

Oh dear, thought the kittens, we shall have to stay here all night. How cold and hungry and miserable we are!

Just then, far below, they saw two small green lights, close together. They were bright and they moved. They stopped at the foot of the tree. Then they began to climb up the tree, higher and higher and higher. What could it be? Then the kittens heard a comfortable voice saying, "It's time you were in bed and asleep." It was their own mother, Mrs. Tabby, and the two green lights were her green eyes, shining in the dark.

First she carried Salt down the tree in her mouth. Then she carried Pepper down the tree in her mouth. The kitchen window was not quite shut and they all squeezed through and snuggled down in their box under the table.

Salt purred and Pepper purred and Mrs. Tabby purred and they purred themselves to sleep.

Charles and Dapple

One day, some new people came to live in the house next door to Charles. He saw the big furniture van stop outside and watched the men carrying in the chairs and carpets and beds. Then he saw them carry a dolls' house through the front door and a tricycle and a low table and chair.

"Oh, Mummy!" shouted Charles, running from the window into the kitchen. "There's a little girl coming to live next door. I've seen some of her things. She has a tricycle just like mine."

Charles did not see the little girl arrive as she came in a car in the evening, when he was going to bed, but next morning, when he was in the garden, he heard her voice. He stood beside the beech hedge and he heard her calling.

"Gee-up! Gee-up! Gee-up!" Then he heard the sound of a whip, crack, crack, and she called again, "Gee-up! Gee-up, Dobbin! Gee-up my fine horse."

Charles listened hard, but he could not hear the sound of hoofs. Could there be a real, live pony next door, galloping round the lawn? If so, it was galloping very quietly. Perhaps the soft grass made it quiet.

Charles climbed on top of the garden roller, which stood by the tool shed, and by standing on tiptoe he could peep over the hedge and look into the next yard. He could see the little girl galloping about on her horse and then he understood why there was no sound of hoofs. This horse had no feet. He was made of a broom-stick and where the bristly part of the broom should be was a horse's head. It looked like a sock stuffed with something.

The little girl galloped up and down, cracking a whip and calling to her horse.

Charles liked the horse's head. It was dark brown with two sharp brown ears and two big round eyes. The little girl saw him peeping over the hedge and she shouted "Whoa! Whoa!" to her horse and stood still.

"Do you like my hobby horse?" she asked. "I call him Dobbin. I've only had him a few days but he already knows his name and stops when I say 'Whoa!' and starts when I say 'Gee-up!' and crack my whip. Would you like to come over here and have a ride?"

"Yes, I would," said Charles. "I can get through the hedge in one place if I wriggle." He soon wriggled through and came out on the other side with bits of twig and leaves in his hair . . . He had a lovely gallop on Dobbin. When they were tired of riding they put Dobbin in the summer house for a stable and gave him a bunch of fresh green grass to munch.

In the afternoon, Charles asked his mother if she could help him to make a hobby horse. They found an old broom in the shed and took the bristly end off. Then his mother got a gray wool sock and Charles stuffed it tightly with rags. His mother sewed on two more bits of sock for ears and two big black buttons for eyes. Then she made some white stitches where the mouth was, to look like teeth. She tied the head very firmly on to the stick with a strong piece of string.

The little girl from next door, whose name was Pat, came and watched.

"Let's have a mane," said Charles. "A nice, long mane."

"I'd like a mane on my horse, too," said Pat. Mother found some thick, black wool and Charles and Pat cut it into pieces the same length and then Mother sewed some on to Charles' horse and some on to Pat's horse.

Charles called his hobby horse Dapple and he and Pat had many good gallops together. Dobbin and Dapple went very well. "Gee-up! Gee-up!" cried Charles and Pat and the horses started off. When they wanted to stop they cried, "Whoa! Whoa!" and the horses stopped at once. They made reins of tape and threaded some curtain rings on them. The rings jingled as the horses galloped, like real harness jingling.

"I'd like a nose-bag for my horse," said Charles. "Horses always eat their dinners out of nose-bags so I want my Dapple to have one. A bag rather like my Useful Bag would do, but it doesn't need to draw up with a string. Dapple likes to put his nose right inside."

Charles' mother made a nose-bag for Dapple and Pat's mother made a nose-bag for Dobbin. When it was dinner time, Charles and Pat filled the nose-bags with grass and hung them round the horses' necks. Then they could munch their food in their stable.

Sometimes, as a treat, Dobbin and Dapple were given an apple or a lump of sugar. If they did not seem hungry just then, can you guess what Charles and Pat did? They crunched the apple themselves. And the sugar, too.

Charles Goes to the Office

"Is it all right for me to come over to your yard to play?" asked Pat, the little girl who lived next door to Charles.

"Sure," said Charles. "Come through the gap." So Pat pushed and squeezed her way through the gap in the beech hedge and came into Charles' garden. Charles was walking up and down, swinging his blue, Useful Bag.

"What's in your Useful Bag today?" asked Pat.

"That's a secret," said Charles. But he added, "You can feel, if you like, and try to guess."

Pat began to pinch and poke the bag with her fingers.

"Is that a clothes-pin? It feels hard and wooden."

"No. That's a thick, thick crayon. It is very special. It writes red one end and blue the other. Feel again."

"A match-box?"

"Yes," said Charles. "It *is* a match-box, but you don't know what's inside."

"I can feel another match-box," said Pat, pinching something and shaking it through the bag. "And soft things like little books. Oh, and hard ones too. Please, please let me look. I won't tell if it is a secret."

Charles always told Pat his secrets in the end because she was his friend.

"We'll go into the summer-house and dump everything out on the table," he said. "Then you can see for yourself. Come along!"

They ran to the summer-house and Charles turned the bag upside down. Out came a queer collection of oddments, match-boxes and note-books and envelopes.

"They are all important office things," said Charles. "Things that men use when they go to the office every day. Here are some clips to clip paper together. Here are lots of little note-books and envelopes. Let's have an office in the summer-house, and do real office work."

Pat thought it was a good idea. "I'll get some things from my house," she said, jumping up. "I'll be back in a minute."

She found another pencil and an eraser. Her mother gave her a roll of plastic tape and she looked in the waste-paper basket for some envelopes. She brought her own scissors, too, and a little pot of paste.

Charles and Pat had a lovely morning. They wrote letters in scribble writing because they could not write real writing yet. They put the letters into envelopes and cut out used stamps and pasted them on with Pat's paste. The letters looked *very* important with a whole row of stamps on, instead of just one in the corner.

"We need a mail-box to drop our letters in," said Pat. "Let's look around the yard and try to find one." They walked around and around the garden, looking everywhere, but they could not see anything that would do. There was a crack between two stones but some bugs lived there, and they might nibble the letters. Suddenly Charles saw a piece of drainpipe that workmen had left near the shed. It was just right, with a hole at the top to drop the letters in.

Charles and Pat often played at office work after this. Charles' mother found a cork and cut an X on it with her penknife. She let them have just a spot of ink in a saucer and they put the cork in the ink and dabbed it hard on the envelopes. It left an inky circle with a cross in the middle. This made their letters look very important indeed.

One morning, Charles and Pat had been very busy in their office. Charles was writing letters in blue crayon and Pat was writing letters in red crayon. They often clipped several pieces of paper together with a paper clip to make a nice fat letter. Then they stuck some stamps on the envelope and dipped the cork in the inky saucer and banged it on, like this—bang! bang!

"I've just written to the President," said Charles. "I've asked him how he feels."

"I've written to the man at the bank," said Pat. "I've said he can send me a sack of money if he wants to."

"Let's mail our letters and then play with our hobby

horses," said Charles. "We've done enough office work for today. Dobbin and Dapple want a gallop."

Just as Pat was about to drop her letter into the mail-box by the shed, a robin flew out and made her jump. "What is he doing down there?" she asked.

"Let me look," said Charles and he bent down. At the bottom of the piece of pipe were twigs and leaves and a few feathers.

"He's building a nest."

"How lovely," said Pat. "Of course we can't mail any more letters now. Let's hide and see if he comes back."

They crouched behind the lilac bushes and watched until they saw the father and the mother robin come with bits of twig in their beaks, and then disappear down the pipe. Then the birds flew off for more. Soon Charles and Pat got pins-and-needles from keeping so still and they ran off to ride their hobby horses.

They were so glad that the robins had chosen to make a nest in their mail-box. They looked forward to seeing the robin babies when the right time came.

Two Surprises

Two children were staying with their grandmother for a week. One was a Big Boy and the other was a Little Girl. They were brother and sister.

Their grandmother's house was full of interesting things to look at. There were china ornaments standing on the mantelpiece and on the shelves and tables as well. The ornaments the children liked best were two china dogs, which sat one each side of the clock. These dogs had red tongues and black spots and gold collars round their necks.

One sunny morning their grandmother said: "Go and play in the yard while I get the dinner ready. See if you can each make me something pretty, for a surprise. You can pick any leaves or flowers or twigs you need."

The Big Boy and the Little Girl ran into the yard and began to look around them.

"I shall be able to make a lovely surprise for Granny," thought the Big Boy. "I am tall and strong and can reach up high. I can climb trees and I have a useful pocket-knife."

"I shall be able to make a lovely surprise for Granny," thought the Little Girl. "I am not very tall or strong, but

I have sharp eyes and some very good ideas."

The Big Boy climbed up the poplar tree and cut off a short, bendy twig with his knife. Then he went to the orchard where the hens and ducks lived and he opened the door of the hen-house and looked under the perches where the hens slept at night. There were some brown speckled feathers that the hens had dropped. He gathered them up in his hand and then he opened the door of the duck-house, where the ducks slept. There he found some more feathers, white ones, as the ducks were white ducks.

He took a piece of string from his pocket and tied all the feathers to the end of the poplar twig, in a bunch. It was like a brush made of feathers.

The Little Girl walked up and down the lawn, picking daisies. Some were all white with yellow middles and some had pink tips to their petals. She liked the pink-tipped ones best. Then she went to the hedge and broke off a prickly branch. It was difficult to break off, but she pulled and pulled and twisted and twisted till it broke.

Then she sat down on the grass and on every prickle she stuck a daisy head. The prickles were like pins and the daisies stayed on them safely. The branch looked very pretty when it was finished, just like a daisy tree. She filled a flower-pot with soil and planted the tiny tree firmly. It looked as if it were growing.

When Grandmother called them in from the yard, the Big Boy and the Little Girl ran to her very quickly.

"See what I have made you," said the Big Boy. "It is a feather brush. You can dust your china dogs with it and your other china ornaments."

"See what I have made you," said the Little Girl. "It is a daisy tree. You can stand it on the table to look pretty."

"What lovely surprises," said Grandmother. "They are the best surprises I have ever had. I shall dust my china dogs with the feather brush, their red tongues and their black spots and their gold collars. When I am tired I shall sit in my rocking-chair and look at my daisy tree."

When I was Small as a Pin

Do you like to hear stories about yourself when you were very small? Charles liked to be told about himself when he slept in a crib and sat in a high chair and had gloves with no fingers like little woolly bags. But sometimes he liked to be told stories about himself that were only pretend ones, made-up ones. He liked to pretend he was once as small as a pin. And his mother pretended too.

One day, Charles said to his mother, "Tell me a story about me, myself. Tell about when I was small as a pin."

"Very well," said his mother. "Where shall I begin?"

"Begin about your handbag," said Charles. "I like that part."

So his mother began. "When you were small as a pin, you always liked to be with me. Perhaps you were afraid of getting lost or stepped on or falling through a crack in the floor. So when I went out shopping, I took you with me, in my handbag."

"In your brown one with the long zipper?" asked Charles.

"Yes, in that very same one. You played with my money and my keys and I could hear you, jingling them inside. Sometimes, for a surprise, I put some special things inside for you, some colored beads and a paper-clip. And you played with them."

"What did you do with me when you were busy washing?"

"I gave you some water in a thimble and you splashed about in it while I washed the clothes."

"What did you do with me when you were cooking?"

"I had to be very careful as you wanted to peep into everything and I was afraid you might fall into the milk or get smothered in the flour. Or perhaps scratch yourself on the nutmeg grater. So I used to lean a wooden spoon against the basin and you climbed up the handle and then slid down. And climbed up and slid down. And climbed up and slid down. You liked sliding so much."

"I still do," said Charles. "And what did I do while you cleaned the house?"

"Oh, I used to carry you around in the pocket of my apron and in every room you had a favorite place. In the dining-room you sat on a little china horse and pretended he was real. In my bedroom you hid in my gloves and I had to hunt for you. And in the bathroom you sat on the shelf and squeezed the toothpaste tube."

"Did I squeeze it hard?"

"Not very, because you were so small."

"What did I do when you ate your dinner?"

"I put you right next to the salt shaker."

"Tell about my bed."

"You slept in a match-box filled with cotton wool, on the table by my bed. Once you ate a whole box of cherry cough drops that I had there."

"Did they give me a pain?"

"Yes, they did. You cried."

"How did I cry?"

"Ee—ee—ee—ee."

"How did you make me happy again?"

"I showed you yourself in a mirror and you looked so funny with your little pin face screwed up and your little pin mouth saying 'ee—ee—ee' that you began to laugh."

"It must have been very comfortable," said Charles, "to be so small and always to be with you."

"But it's much nicer now," said his mother. "We can talk now and play together and I'm not afraid of losing you. You couldn't slip between the floor-boards now."

"Or fall into the milk pitcher."

"Or get stepped on."

"And I'll never, never be lost," said Charles. "If I even *felt* lost for a minute I could always say my name and where I lived. Then someone would take me home."

"So you could. Will you say them to me?"

"I'm Charles Cox and I live at fourteen-forty Atlantic Avenue, Centerville."

That was a useful thing to know, wasn't it? Do you know your name and address like Charles?

Granny-in-the-Country

Charles was very lucky because he had two grandmothers. One lived by the sea and he called her "granny-by-the-sea." The other lived in the country and he called her "granny-in-the-country." Sometimes he went with his mother to visit his grannies and sometimes he stayed all by himself for a few days.

Granny-in-the-country lived in a cottage. She had a yard where Charles could play and there was a road with green hedges just outside the gate. His mother took him by train to the nearest station and there granny met him. She had an old-fashioned little pony cart outside, drawn by Peggy the pony, and she lifted Charles' suitcase inside.

Then Charles, carrying his Useful Bag himself, climbed up and sat beside her.

"Gee-up, Peggy pony," said granny. "Gee-up!" and Peggy tossed her head and set off at a gentle clip-clop, clip-clop, along the lane.

"May I hold the reins, please?" asked Charles.

"Yes, for a little while," said granny and Charles sat up very straight and still, holding the leather reins tightly. The leather had a smell like new shoes.

When they got to the cottage, Charles climbed down from the cart and ran up the path, swinging his Useful Bag by the strings. The cottage was exactly as he remembered. The door stood open, with a horse-shoe nailed on it for a knocker. There was a fire burning and the kettle was singing. There was a smell of fresh gingerbread. Charles hung his bag on the back of a chair and ran outside again.

"Granny! Granny! Can I give Peggy pony a drink of water?"

"Yes," said granny, who was undoing Peggy's harness. "I'll help you."

There was a well near the back door with a heavy cover over the top. Granny moved the cover and helped Charles to turn the handle so that the bucket, on the end of the rope, went down, down, down into the water. It made a splash when it got there. Winding the handle back again was difficult now there was a heavy bucket of water to be lifted, but they managed it between them. They gave Peggy a drink and she dipped her soft nose in and gulped the cool water. When she had had enough she lifted her head and whinnied. Charles tried to whinny back but he did not do it very well.

There was hot gingerbread for Charles and milk in a special mug, with daisies painted round it. At the very bottom, on the inside, was the picture of a cow. As Charles drank, he watched for the picture of the cow to appear. When he was near the bottom he saw first her

head and then her back and then her legs. This made it easy to finish every drop. He never left any of his milk when he was staying with granny-in-the-country.

When Charles was in bed he asked granny to tell him just one little story before he went to sleep. "Of course I will," said granny. "Which story do you want to hear?"

"Please tell about Peggy pony in the snow," said Charles. So granny began:

"One wintry day when the snow was on the ground, I went to the stable to give Peggy pony her breakfast. 'Here's a nice hot breakfast for you,' I said, as I came down the path. Then I saw that the stable door was wide open and I looked inside and saw the straw on the floor, but no Peggy pony. Where could she be on such a cold frosty morning? Had a thief come in the night and stolen her away?

"Then I saw a trail of hoof-marks in the snow and I followed the hoof-marks out of the gate and along the road and over the bridge and past the post office. Then they swung round into the blacksmith's forge and as I followed them I heard the clang—clang—clang of the blacksmith's hammer and I heard something else too. I heard Peggy pony's whinny. And there stood Peggy inside the forge, holding up one of her back feet so patiently while the blacksmith fitted a bright new shoe on it.

" 'Good girl! Good girl, your Peggy!' said the blacksmith, smiling. 'I heard her whinnying outside in the snow and I opened my door and in she trotted. What can I do for you? I asked and she held up her foot to show that she'd cast a shoe. So I've made her a new one, as you can see.'

"Wasn't that clever of Peggy pony? Then I got on her back and paid the blacksmith for the new shoe and we rode home. Then Peggy had her breakfast rather late.

"When the snow melted, I found the old shoe she had lost by the gate."

"Is it the one nailed on the door for a knocker?" asked

Charles sleepily.

"Yes, the very same one. And when she casts another shoe you shall have it to nail on *your* door, at home."

By this time Charles was very nearly asleep but as he knew every word of the story by heart it did not matter. Granny would tell him the same story the next night and the next night and the one after that, until he asked for a new one.

Granny-by-the-Sea

You have already heard a story about "granny-in-the-country" and her Peggy pony. Today you can hear one about "granny-by-the-sea".

Charles liked staying by the sea with granny. He liked everything there, the house, the garden, granny's ginger cat, and the brown sugar he was given to sprinkle over his oatmeal in the morning. But of course the best thing of all was the sea itself. He wanted to spend every minute on the beach and he thought that shopping or going for a walk was a waste of time.

The first time Charles saw the sea he was only two years old and he ran right into the water, before anyone could catch him, and soaked his new brown sandals and his shorts and half his blouse as well! Now he was four, he was too sensible to get wet with all his clothes on. He waited till he was wearing his bathing suit, or at least till he had taken off his shoes and socks.

Granny knew just how much Charles liked being on the beach. When he arrived, with his luggage, and his Useful Bag slung over one shoulder, she never bothered about unpacking and putting things in drawers straight away. She gave him a glass of milk and then they both put on their sun hats and went down the steep cliff path to the beach. Granny came slowly behind holding on to the wooden railing at the side, but Charles ran like the wind. When he got to the bottom of the path there were three steps and he took a great, big, flying jump down these and landed in the soft sand which filled his shoes. But this did not matter as he just sat down plomp and took off his shoes and socks and left them lying there and ran on towards the water's edge. Granny, coming along behind, picked up the shoes and socks and stuffed them in the beach bag with the towel and the spare jersey and the other such things she kept there.

The sea was always a little colder than Charles expected.

He said "O—oh! O—oh!" with surprise when the cold, clear waves washed over his feet and ankles. "O—oh! O—oh!"

The sand by the edge of the sea was damp and dark and firm while the sand higher up the beach, where granny sat, was dry and pale and powdery. There were two games

Charles liked to play with sand, one game with the damp sand and one with the dry. I will tell you what he did with the damp sand first.

He got his spade and bucket from granny, filled his bucket full of sand, well pressed down, and he turned the bucket upside down. He patted the bottom of it with his spade, like this—tap! tap! tap! Then, very carefully, he lifted up the bucket and there stood a perfect sand castle, just the size of the bucket. Charles made one castle for granny and one for mother and one for daddy and one for his other granny and one for himself. That was five. They stood in a row and he put a special thing on each to make it pretty. One had a clam shell. One had a white stone. One had some green seaweed. One had a pink shell. His own was very grand with a paper flag on a stick. Granny made the flag out of an envelope and Charles put it on the stick.

Now I will tell you about the other game Charles played with the dry, powdery sand. He scooped a hollow in the sand with his hands and lay down in it. "Please bury me," he said to granny, and if she was not too busy knitting or writing letters she always did.

First she buried his legs. His toes disappeared and his feet and his knees. Then his shorts disappeared and his chest and his arms and his neck. There was only his head peeping out.

"Bury my face, please bury my face," begged Charles. But granny always said: "No dear, not your face. You would get sand in your eyes and that would hurt. And sand in your nose and that would tickle. We'll just leave your face showing."

Charles had to keep as still as a stone. If he moved the least, tiniest bit a toe would poke through the sand or a knee or a finger. He could not turn his head, so all he could see was some blue sky and a white cloud sailing across.

"It's time to go now," said granny.

"But I can't move," said Charles. "I can't move at all. I'll never be able to move again."

"I'm sorry to hear that," said granny, not at all worried because she knew Charles was pretending.

"I'll have to stay here all night," went on Charles. "And all tomorrow. And the next day and the next."

"What will you do when the tide comes up and washes over you?" asked granny.

"Jump up like a jack-in-the-box!" shouted Charles, leaping up in the air and scattering sand everywhere.

"Gracious me!" said granny. "You gave me a terrible fright!" and she fanned herself with her knitting pattern. Charles gave her a hug and then she wasn't frightened any more and they went up the beach together, up the three steps and up the steep cliff path towards home. Charles held granny's hand all the way because he was tired and it was nearly his bedtime.

Mr. Moon

One morning, the postman knocked on the door of the house where Charles lived. "Rat-atat-tat!" Charles ran to the door and picked a letter off the mat. "Oh, it's for me!" he cried, running into the kitchen. "Mummy, it *is* for me, isn't it?"

Charles could not read yet, but he knew what C for

Charles looked like and he knew the shape of the curly S at the end of his name.

"Yes," said his mother. "It says MASTER CHARLES COX on the envelope."

"Please read it to me now," said Charles, "this very minute. Who is it from?"

"It is from old Miss Winter." Now Miss Winter was an old lady who lived nearby and often waved to Charles when he rode past on his tricycle. This is what the letter said:

DEAR CHARLES,

I am going away for the night to see my sister and I do not want to leave Mr. Moon alone in the house. May he stay with you, please? I will bring him round this morning and pick him up tomorrow afternoon.

I hope he will behave himself.

With love from
Miss Winter.

"Oh, Mother, do say he can come!" begged Charles.

"He can come if you want him," replied Mother.

"Of course I want him. What do you think he can be? A cat? Or a dog? Or a squirrel? Or a rabbit?"

His mother said "We'll have to wait and see."

Charles kept wondering about Mr. Moon while he ate his breakfast. Who could he be? What could he be? What would happen if he didn't behave himself?

Soon after breakfast there was another knock on the door. Charles ran to open it. At first he thought there was no one there and then he saw, on the porch, a small, brown suitcase with a strap round it. And on the suitcase sat Mr. Moon.

Mr. Moon wasn't a cat or a dog or a squirrel or a rabbit. He was a teddy bear, the biggest teddy bear Charles had ever seen. He was nearly as big as Charles himself. He wore a red coat and blue trousers. Charles took him in his arms.

"Carry Mr. Moon upstairs and unpack for him," suggested Mother. "There is one empty drawer in your chest of drawers. You can put his things in there."

So Charles took Mr. Moon upstairs and his suitcase as well, and he sat the teddy bear in a chair while he undid the strap around the case. Mr. Moon sat up beautifully, leaning against the back of the chair with his legs straight out in front of him. He looked very pleased.

Charles unpacked the bag and put the things in the drawer. Mr. Moon had brought all he could possibly want for the night. Striped red and white pajamas. A brush and comb. Two clean handkerchiefs with M in

the corner. A straw hat. A box of hard candies. At the very bottom of the suitcase was a green umbrella.

Charles spent a long time arranging Mr. Moon's things and playing with the green umbrella. Then he took Mr. Moon out into the garden and put him in a deck chair with the umbrella open to shade his face. He seemed quite happy, sitting there and staring in front of him.

When Charles rested after dinner, Mr. Moon lay on the bed too and Charles told him a story about three little pigs. Mr. Moon liked being told stories.

They went into the park later in the afternoon, with mother. Charles found an acorn pipe for Mr. Moon to smoke and a daisy to put in his buttonhole.

When it was bedtime, Charles prepared a dolls' cradle he had for Mr. Moon to sleep in. But Mr. Moon had made up his mind to be awkward. First he stuck his legs out at the bottom, untucking the blankets. Then he poked an arm up in the air. Then he poked the other arm out at the side. And he looked most annoyed about something.

"Oh my!" said Charles. "Mr. Moon is SO cross. He won't go to bed nicely."

"I expect he is cross because you have forgotten his pajamas," said Mother.

"How silly I am," cried Charles, and he took off Mr. Moon's red jacket and blue trousers and put on his striped pajamas. Then he took the brush and comb from the drawer and began to smooth Mr. Moon's furry head.

He brushed and combed and brushed and combed very gently but it made little difference. Then he tucked Mr. Moon into bed again. But Mr. Moon leaned over one side of the cradle and upset it, pillow and bed-clothes and himself and all, out on to the floor.

"He doesn't like this cradle," said Charles. "He thinks it is babyish. He wants a bed like mine. What can I use for a bed for him?"

"This box the groceries came in might do," suggested mother. They put a cushion in the box and made it cozy with a blanket Charles had had when he was little. Mr. Moon behaved beautifully. He did not poke his toes out or his arms. He lay still and good as could be.

"Goodnight, Mr. Moon," said Charles. "Call me if you want anything in the night."

But Mr. Moon slept well. Neither he nor Charles moved till it was morning.

Charles got up the minute he was called, as he wanted to dress Mr. Moon. He managed the three buttons on the jacket and the suspenders on his blue trousers.

Charles was sorry when Miss Winter called to take Mr. Moon home.

"Has he behaved himself?" she asked.

"Yes," said Charles. "He has been the best teddy bear in the world," and he gave him a hug. "May he come again one day?"

"Yes, if you ask him," said Miss Winter, while Charles packed the suitcase.

"Mr. Moon is not fond of candy," said Miss Winter. "He wants you to keep his box of goodies as a present."

So Charles kept the little candies for himself. They were tiny colored ones called "Dolly Mixture".

Mr. Moon comes for Christmas

Charles and Mr. Moon had such a good time together that Charles hoped Mr. Moon would come again. Well, he *did* come again and this story tells you about the visit.

Miss Winter was going away at Christmas to stay with her sister and she did not want to leave Mr. Moon alone in the house, so she asked Charles if he could spend Christmas with him.

"Of course he can," said Charles. "What a lovely idea! I'll take great care of him. Does he know about Christmas?"

"He may have forgotten," said Miss Winter. "Last Christmas he was such a very small teddy bear. You will have to tell him again."

"I will," said Charles. "I'll explain it all to him, Christmas trees and carols and candles and everything."

Mr. Moon arrived with his brown suitcase and Charles unpacked for him. He brought a brush and comb and the same red and white striped pajamas as before. And his green umbrella. His straw hat and one woolly white sock. Mr. Moon looked puzzled when he saw Charles holding up just one sock. He wondered where the other one could be.

"Don't worry, Mr. Moon," said Charles. "This is your Christmas sock. You must hang it at the foot of your bed tonight and Santa Claus will come and fill it with toys. It will be bursting with nice things when you wake up in the morning."

Mr. Moon looked just a little puzzled.

"Perhaps you don't quite remember about Santa Claus," suggested Charles kindly. "He is a jolly old man with a white beard and rosy cheeks. He wears a red cloak with a hood on it and white fur round the edge of the hood. He carries a great, big, ENORMOUS sack of toys on his back and rides along on a sleigh pulled by reindeer. Children never really see him because he comes when they are asleep, but there are pictures of him in some of my books."

Charles brought a book from the bookcase and turned over the pages till he came to a picture of Santa in his sleigh. It was almost Charles' favorite picture. The snowflakes were whirling through the air, but Santa Claus looked snug and warm in his red hood. The sack was so full that some of the toys poked out at the top. Charles could see the end of a flag and the stick of a drum and a bit of a silver trumpet. The reindeer had bells on their harness and they were running so fast that their feet hardly touched the ground. They looked as if they were flying.

Mr. Moon was very interested. He leaned forward till his black nose touched the page. Perhaps he wanted to ride on the sleigh. Or perhaps he was wondering what Santa would bring him.

The day passed very quickly and after dinner they all sang carols while mother played the piano. Charles knew bits of a great many carols.

Mr. Moon sat on top of the piano and listened.

When Charles was in his blue and white pajamas and Mr. Moon was in his red and white ones, Charles' mother tucked them both up in their beds. Mr. Moon's box bed was close beside Charles'. She hung Mr. Moon's woolly white sock at the foot of his bed and Charles' bigger, brown sock at the foot of his.

"Go to sleep as soon as you can," she said, "because the sooner you get to sleep the sooner Christmas morning will come."

"I'm going to stay awake and see Santa Claus,"

whispered Charles to Mr. Moon. "I've always wanted to see him and hear the reindeer's bells."

Mr. Moon said nothing.

"I'm very sleepy," whispered Charles, a little later. "I think I'll just have a little nap. I'm sure to wake up when the sleigh bells ring."

But do you think he did wake up? No, he never

opened his eyes till it was morning. Before he put on the light, he crawled to the foot of his bed and felt his stocking. It wasn't thin and empty any longer; it was fat and full. He reached an arm over the side of the bed and touched Mr. Moon's white sock. That was full too.

"Wake up, Mr. Moon," shouted Charles. "A happy Christmas!" And he jumped out of bed and switched on the light. Then he put on his bathrobe as his mother had told him and began to unpack his stocking. "It's the best stocking I've ever had! The best stocking in the world!" said Charles, carefully unpacking his presents, one by one. There was something to eat—a rosy apple. Something to make a noise with—a tiny mouth organ. Something to play with—some glass marbles. And a surprise, wrapped up. This surprise was a tiny teddy bear made of wool, no bigger than his little finger, with a safety-pin fixed at the back so it could be pinned on to his jersey.

Then Charles helped Mr. Moon to unpack his Christmas sock. Santa must have taken great care in choosing his presents because they were all so small and just right for a teddy bear. A plaid muffler. A bar of chocolate. A cup and saucer not much bigger than an acorn.

When mother came in to wish them a happy Christmas they were both sitting up in Charles' bed and Charles was blowing his mouth organ. "I'm playing 'Jingle Bells'," he said. "Did you guess? Is it nearly right?"

"Nearly," smiled Mother. "Anyhow, it sounds just like Christmas."

Jeremy and his Noah's Ark

One day, a little boy called Jeremy decided he would play with his Noah's Ark. It was kept on a high shelf in the toy cupboard, but he stood on a wooden stool and stretched up, up, till he could just reach it. Then he stepped down from the stool and carried the Noah's Ark very, very carefully to the table.

It was an old Noah's Ark, much, much older than Jeremy who was only four. It had belonged to Jeremy's father when *he* was a little boy. Jeremy's father must have been very careful and gentle as not one of the animals was badly broken. There was a chip off one camel's hump and a black, spotted pig had to stand on three legs instead of four, but that was all. And of course some of the bright paint had faded.

The Noah's Ark was shaped like a boat, with a house inside it. The boat part was green, with wavy lines running round to look like waves of water. The house part was white, with four square windows. The roof was red, with a white dove painted on the top. The roof lifted right off, like the lid of a box, and Jeremy could dive his hand inside and take out the animals.

Jeremy began to take out the animals in pairs, two by two. He stood two yellow lions side by side. Two striped tigers side by side. Then two spotted leopards and two white sheep. Soon there was a long, long line of animals winding across the table.

There were two Noah's Ark people as well as the animals, both with flat, round hats and blue coats. They were Mr. and Mrs. Noah. It was easy to tell which was which, as Mr. Noah had a white beard and carried a stick. Jeremy put Mr. Noah at the back, to drive the animals along and he put Mrs. Noah at the front, to lead them in the right way.

But today there seemed to be another person inside the Ark, as well as Mr. and Mrs. Noah. Whoever could it be? Jeremy lifted the strange person out and found that it was a small green Elf.

The small green Elf wriggled out of Jeremy's hand and took off his pointed green hat and said:

"Good afternoon, Boy."

"Good afternoon, Elf," said Jeremy. "What are you doing in my Noah's Ark?"

"I was hiding there," said the small, green Elf. "I hoped you would soon want to play with the Noah's Ark and then you would find me inside. I've always wanted to have a ride on an elephant, like children do at the zoo. Could I have a ride on one of your elephants, please?"

"Yes, you may," said Jeremy. "I'll lift you on to his back and give you a ride up and down the table."

So he lifted the Elf on to the back of one of the elephants and the Elf sat very straight and still, holding on to the elephant's big gray ears. Jeremy made the elephant walk to the far end of the table and back again. Then he made the elephant run a little and the Elf had to hold on very tightly with both hands.

"That was wonderful!" said the Elf. "Simply wonderful! May I ride on one of your camels?"

"Yes," said Jeremy, "you may." And he put the small green Elf on the top of the camel's hump and made the camel walk to the far end of the table and back.

"Make him run, please," said the Elf, and Jeremy made the camel run and the Elf clung on tightly and laughed as he went bumpety-bump, bumpety-bump.

"Thank you very much for the rides," said the Elf. "I

must go home now. Goodby!" He jumped on to the window-sill and climbed down the ivy and disappeared.

Jeremy put his animals back into the Ark, two by two. Two yellow lions. Two striped tigers. Two spotted leopards. Two white sheep and all the others. Then he saw the Elf's green, pointed hat on the table. He had left it behind by mistake.

"I'll let Mrs. Noah have it till the Elf comes back," thought Jeremy, and he perched the pointed hat on top of Mrs. Noah's flat one. It was very smart indeed.

Mrs. Noah looked pleased and I am sure she was pleased, too, because ladies usually like to have new hats.

The small green Elf hasn't come back for his hat yet, so Mrs. Noah is still wearing it. Do you think he has forgotten all about it? Or perhaps he has another one at home.

What will it Grow Into?

Charles had a great many little games and "pretends" that he played only with his mother. No one else knew about them. They were secret and special. There was one little game they often played at bed-time, when Charles' mother had kissed him and tucked him up for the night. This was what they did.

At the very last minute, before the light was turned off, Charles poked one hand out from under the warm bedclothes and his mother put a kiss in it. Then he curled his fingers over the kiss just as though she had put a tiny bead there, or an acorn or a sweet. Then his mother asked: "What will it grow into by the morning?"

Charles sometimes said, "a pink tulip" or "an apple tree" or even "a lamp-post" or "a peacock". While he was thinking about the pink tulip or the apple tree or the lamp-post or the peacock, he usually fell fast asleep.

One night, when his mother had put the kiss inside his hand and he had curled his fingers safely over it, she asked, "What will it grow into by the morning?" and he said, "An orange tree covered with oranges."

While he was thinking how nice that would be, he fell asleep and had a dream about oranges. I will tell you what happened in the dream.

Charles dreamed he was standing under a big tree covered with dark green leaves and bright oranges. There were hundreds and hundreds of oranges, shining like baubles on a Christmas tree. "How I wish I could have one to eat," thought Charles. "I'll ask mother to peel it and divide it into a lot of little pigs. No, I think I'll have a hole in one end and put a lump of sugar in the hole and suck and suck and suck till all the juice is gone. Or I shall have it cut in two halves and then I'll yum all around the edge and get my chin sticky with juice."

But he could not do any of these nice things because the tree was very tall and too difficult to climb. What a pity!

He looked at the ground under the tree to see if an orange had fallen off, but he could not find one anywhere.

Just then he heard a chattering noise and he looked up and there, on one of the branches, was a little black monkey. The little black monkey was chattering rather crossly, ch—ch—chtt—, ch—ch—chtt.

"Mr. Monkey," said Charles politely, "will you please throw me just one of those lovely oranges?"

"No," said the monkey. "I want them ALL for myself. Ch—ch—chtt."

"Couldn't you spare a little tiny one?"

"No," said the monkey again. "I want the little tiny ones AND the big ones. I want them ALL!"

"You're a very greedy monkey," said Charles. "You'll be sick if you eat all those oranges. Very sick indeed."

"Oh no I shan't," snapped the little monkey. "Nothing ever makes me sick. Ch—ch—chtt."

Charles wanted an orange very badly and when he saw the monkey pick one for himself and begin to nibble it, he wanted one more than ever. Then he had a good idea.

"Mr. Monkey," he shouted loudly. "You're a silly billy."

"I'm not," shouted back the monkey. "My name isn't Billy and I'm not silly. Ch—ch—chtt."

"You are a silly billy," went on Charles. "You're so silly you couldn't hit me if you tried!"

"I could. Easy as pie!" and the monkey picked another orange and threw it at Charles. And then he threw another. And another. And another, till the ground was littered with oranges. But he did not hit Charles once because Charles was dodging about, here, there and everywhere, and never kept still a second.

When the monkey was tired of throwing oranges at

Charles, he sat still and waved his thin little arms and chattered with rage, ch—ch—chtt.

Charles picked up a large golden orange and he was just going to eat it when he heard his mother's voice saying, "Time to wake up, Charles, and here's your orange juice."

So Charles opened his eyes and looked at his mother with the glass of orange juice in her hand and he wondered, just for a minute, where the orange tree had gone to and the little black monkey.

"I've had a dream," he said while his mother drew back the curtains, "a lovely dream about oranges," and he told her all about it while he sipped his orange juice.

That was a nice dream to have, wasn't it? And it was a good ending, too, for Charles to wake up and have REAL orange juice to drink.

Brother Mouse and Sister Mouse

Once upon a time there were two little mice. They were brother and sister and they lived together on the beach in a bath-house. This sounds a very odd place for two little mice to live, but they were really quite comfortable. They had a snug hole in a corner, between two boards.

What could they find to eat, living on the beach? Well, they could not eat fishy, salty things like seaweed and shrimps, because mice do not care for fishy, salty tastes. They ate delicious crumbs of cake and cookies and sandwiches.

Where did they find these delicious crumbs? They were dropped by the children and grown-ups who used the bath-house to undress in before they had a swim, and to dress in afterwards. When the children came running and laughing and shivering up from the sea, their mothers nearly always said, "Here's a nice cinnamon bun, dear, to eat while you are getting dressed." Or, "Here is a sandwich—or a cookie—or a square of chocolate."

The children always dropped crumbs as they ate and the little mice ran out of their hole, when no one was looking, and gobbled them up. All through the summer the little mice kept fat and contented with their meals of crumbs, but when the summer was over, the children went back to their homes and it was much too cold to go swimming. The man who owned the bath-house locked it up for the winter and went away too.

Poor little mice, how cold and hungry they felt. They

crept over the pebbles and sand and tried to nibble bits of seaweed, but it was so salty that they had to spit it out. One day, Brother Mouse found half a coconut at the edge of the sea. It was round and brown, rather like a bowl.

"I have an idea," said Brother Mouse. "Find me two straight pieces of wood, Sister, about the same size."

Sister Mouse hunted here and there and found two strong straight sticks. Then Brother Mouse jumped inside the half coconut and took a stick in each paw and said:

"Look, Sister! This is our boat and these are our oars to row with. Jump in beside me and let's go for a sail. We may find somewhere else to live in a place across the sea."

Sister Mouse was very frightened, but she did not want to be left behind, so she jumped in beside Brother Mouse. Just then a big wave came rushing in, whoosh—whoosh—and in a moment the little round boat was afloat.

Oh, how the boat rolled and tossed, up—up—up—on one wave. Then down—down—down—on the next. UP—d-o-o-o-w-n! UP—d-o-o-o-w-n! UP—d-o-o-o-w-n!

Sister Mouse began to feel sick but Brother Mouse was too busy with the oars to think of anything else. Soon they got used to being rolled and tossed about and they began to enjoy themselves. They could see nothing but sky and sea, blue sky above and green waves all round with foamy white tips. They floated on for a very long time and they began to wonder if they ever *would* reach land. Their legs were stiff with sitting still so long and Brother Mouse's arms ached with tugging at the oars.

Suddenly they saw something tall sticking up out of the water.

"Land ahead!" shouted Brother Mouse. "Land ahead!"

Then the boat bumped into the tall thing and stopped moving.

The tall thing was a huge wooden post. "Let's climb up the post and stretch our legs," said Sister Mouse. So they climbed up the post which was slippery with wet, green seaweed and prickly with sharp, pointed shells.

When they were at the top there was a wooden floor to walk on.

"Oh!" sighed Sister Mouse. "What a lovely smell!"

"Oh!" sighed Brother Mouse, "I *am* hungry!"

The smell was a mixture of toast and coffee and sausages and spice cake. It came from a large house nearby.

The two little mice crept in through the door, which happened to be open, and found a comfortable home in a hole in a dark corner. They learned that the house was a café at the end of a pier and the wooden post they had climbed up was part of the pier.

The café made a very good home. It was open all the year round, winter and summer, and there was always plenty of food and plenty of crumbs.

Once, someone said to the lady who sold the food: "I saw a mouse under the table. You must buy a mouse-trap and catch him." But the lady said: "Mice? What an idea! Whoever heard of mice living at the end of a pier?"

Brother Mouse and Sister Mouse hugged each other in their safe little corner and felt glad they had left the cold bath-house on the beach and floated in their coconut boat to this lovely, comfortable place.

Crackers the Squirrel

Once upon a time, there was a family of squirrels who lived in a beech tree. There was a father squirrel and a mother squirrel and three little squirrels. They had a very happy life in the beech tree, playing among the branches. In the autumn, when the beech-nuts were ripe, they ate as many as they wanted and hid the rest in holes at the foot of the tree, to eat later on.

Near the beech tree was a house and the little squirrels, if they crept to the tip of a long, bendy branch, could jump on to one of the window-sills. This window belonged to the nursery. The squirrels pressed their furry, whiskery faces against the glass and looked inside. They saw a family of children eating or playing or listening to the wireless.

One of the squirrels was called Crackers because he was good at cracking nuts. He spent hours peeping in the window. He looked at everything in the room, but best of all, he liked the shelf where the toy animals sat. There was a whole row of them: a teddy bear, a panda, a rabbit with velvet ears, a yellow duck and a big white elephant.

He often wished he were a toy squirrel instead of a live one and could sit on the shelf with the other toy animals. It looked so cozy in the room with the bright fire and the warm carpet on the floor and the pictures on the walls—much nicer than being out of doors in the wind and the cold.

One afternoon, Crackers crept along the bendy branch and jumped on to the window-sill. The nursery was very quiet as the children had gone out to tea. The fire was blazing brightly and he could see the shelf of toy animals. The window was open a little way and he squeezed through and sprang on to the floor. He ran across the room—climbed on the back of a chair—and jumped on to the shelf.

There was a space between the teddy bear and the elephant and he sat down in the space, feeling very pleased with himself. But the teddy bear and the elephant did not look very pleased. They frowned and turned their backs on him. Presently the teddy bear growled:

"What shop did you come from?"

"I didn't come from a shop," said Crackers. "I came from the beech tree."

"WE all came from shops," said the other animals. "Large, important shops with counters and glass cases and telephones."

"How much did you cost?" asked the white elephant.

"I don't think I cost anything," said Crackers.

"WE all cost a lot of money," said the other animals. "WE are very expensive indeed."

"What are you stuffed with?" asked the panda.

"I don't know. I don't think I am stuffed with anything. I'm just squirrel all the way through."

"WE are all stuffed with the very best stuffing," said all the other animals.

Crackers hung his head. He was sorry he was such a queer creature with no regular stuffing.

"Do sit still!" grumbled the yellow duck. "We never fidget on this shelf."

"Can't you stop sniffing?" complained the rabbit with velvet ears. "I have such good ears that I can hear every sniff."

Crackers tried to sit very still indeed and not to fidget or sniff. He even tried not to breathe, but he had to take a breath in the end. He felt uncomfortable. He had a tickle at the back of his neck and pins-and-needles in one foot.

Just then a black cat came into the room. The other animals took no notice at all. They did not even turn their heads. But Crackers felt cold shivers go up and down his back. His teeth began to chatter and his whiskers trembled. He wished he were in the beech tree with his mother.

"Is it a nice cat?" he whispered to the teddy bear.

"It's just an ordinary cat," said the teddy bear. "She never takes any notice of us. Why should she?"

But the cat was behaving in a strange way. She sniffed and stretched her neck and her green eyes searched every corner of the nursery. Then she jumped on to a chair and stared at the shelf of toy animals. She stared straight at Crackers. She smiled and showed her white, pointed teeth. Then she gave a deep, hungry growl— — — —.

The growl was too much for Crackers. He gave a leap off the shelf—on to the table—then on to the window-sill —through the window—and on to the bendy branch. Before you could crack a nut, he was safe in the nest with his mother and father and the other little squirrels.

Crackers never even looked through the nursery window again. He did not want to be a stuffed animal and sit still all the while, and he did not want ever to see the black cat again with her green eyes and white, pointed teeth.

He was very glad he was a live squirrel and lived in a beech tree.

The Glass Bird

At night, when everyone had gone to bed, the Christmas tree woke up. The dark green branches swayed from side to side, and the little bells rang, and the paper chains rustled. A silver bugle blew "Toot! Toot! Toot!" and two wooden drum sticks beat "Tum! Tum! Tum!" on the drum. The Fairy Doll on the topmost bough rose on her toes and turned round and round, waving her wand till the star at the end twinkled like a real star.

There was a glass bird on the Christmas tree. She was very pretty with silver wings and a silver tail. Her feet and her beak were red. She spread her silver wings and flew about the room, pecking at the berries of the holly. Sometimes she rested on the back of a chair or on the bookcase. She was happy, but she did not sing. There was no other bird to sing to.

Once, when she was flying near the mantelpiece, she perched on the clock and listened to its steady "Tick-tock! Tick-tock!" There was a mirror hanging over the clock and she saw, in the clear glass, a wonderful sight. It was a pretty little bird with silver wings and a silver tail, and a red beak and red feet.

"Now I shall have a companion," she said. "Now I shall have someone to talk to in the long winter evenings."

She sang, "Sweet! Sweet!" and the bird in the mirror sang "Sweet! Sweet!" back again.

She bowed her silver head and spread her silver wings, and the bird in the mirror did the same.

When it was time for the toys to go back to their places on the tree, ready for the next day, the silver bird would not leave the mantelpiece.

"Come back!" rapped the drum. "Tum-tum-tum!"

"Come back!" blew the bugle. "Toot! Toot! Toot!"

"Come back!" said the Fairy Doll. "It is time to take your place."

"Come back!" said the empty branch. "Come back and

perch on me!" But the glass bird shook her head.

"I shall never come back," she said. "I shall stay where I am always, with my new friend."

When the clock struck twelve, someone in a red coat, with a white beard and a sack of toys on his back, came into the house. "Oh Santa Claus, do help us!" begged all the toys on the tree. "The glass bird won't come and perch on her branch. She is looking at herself in the mirror. She thinks her reflection is another bird and she says she will stay there always and never come back."

"Little bird, come back to your branch," said Santa Claus gently. "The tree looks so much better if you are in your place. Come back, little bird."

"Never! Never! Never!" whistled the glass bird. "I will never leave my new friend."

"There is only one thing to do," said Santa Claus. "We must get another glass bird and put it on the branch to sit beside her. But how are we to get one? My sack is full to bursting, but there isn't another bird among the things. I have one in my workshop in the Land of Ice and Snow, but that is hundreds of miles away. My reindeer cannot get there and back by morning."

"I will fetch the glass bird," said a red airplane which was hanging on the tree. "I can get there and back in no time."

"Thank you, red airplane," said Santa Claus. "You will find the glass bird on a shelf just inside the door of my workshop."

"How shall I find your workshop?" asked the red airplane.

"It is covered with holly and mistletoe, and there is a lantern hanging outside," said Santa Claus, unfastening the string that held the airplane to the branch. Then he opened a window. The propellers began to whizz round and the engine began to roar and the pilot, in his helmet and goggles, flew the plane out of the window towards the north.

Santa Claus went back to his sleigh and drove away because he had work to do.

It was nearly morning when the red airplane flew back, bringing the glass bird.

"See what I have brought back from the Land of Ice and Snow," said the pilot, and the glass bird stopped looking at herself in the mirror and turned her head and saw the new bird. She flew to meet him and the two birds bowed their heads and spread their wings and sang a song of welcome.

Then they sat side by side, on the empty branch that was waiting for them.

"Three cheers!" blew the bugle. "Toot! Toot! Toot!"

"All is well," said the Fairy Doll, waving her wand.

When the candles were lit on Christmas Day and the children gathered round to watch and have their presents, they all said:

"How pretty the two glass birds are! They look so friendly, sitting side by side on the same branch."

Mollie Under the Apple Tree

One day, a little girl called Mollie was playing in the yard. She was lying in the long grass under the apple tree. It was very quiet, because there was no one to make a noise. She could just hear a bird saying, "Tweet! Tweet! Tweet!" And a bee saying, "Buzz! Buzz! Buzz!" And a pony trotting down the lane, Trit-trot! Trit-trot! Trit-trot!

Presently she heard another sound, like very small feet marching along. They went pit-pat, pit-pat, pit-pat. Then, between the tall grasses, came some tiny little men. They were no bigger than Mollie's little finger. Each one carried

something to dig with. One had a spade. One had a fork. Another had a trowel. And each carried a sack on his back.

They all had white beards and they looked SO cross and tired. Their faces were red and hot and they grumbled as

they walked along.

"I'm SO hot," said one.

"I'm SO tired," said another.

"I'm SO cross," said the next.

"I can't dig any more," said the one after that, and they all sighed together like this: Sigh! Sigh! Sigh!

"What are you digging for?" asked Mollie.

"We are digging for treasure to give to our King," said one. "We want to find pretty things to put in our sacks."

"Have you found any treasure?" asked Mollie.

"No, we haven't. That's why we're so tired and cross."

Mollie felt very sorry for them. "Sit down and rest," she said. "It is cool under this apple tree."

So the little men laid their spades and forks and trowels on the ground. They took off their sacks and sat down. They all took out red bandana handkerchiefs and wiped their hot faces. Then they closed their eyes and had a nice, comfortable doze. While they were resting, Mollie ran indoors and fetched her bead-box. It was full of beads of all kinds, big ones and little ones, colored ones and plain ones. She found a patch of soft soil and buried some of the beads, not very deeply. She buried the prettiest, the ones that shone like real jewels.

When the little men woke, they yawned and picked up their empty sacks and their spades and forks and trowels.

"Do you know where there is any treasure?" they asked Mollie.

Mollie led them to the patch of soft soil and said, "Why not try here?"

The little men began to dig and soon one called out, "I've found some red treasure." And another called out, "I've found some blue treasure." And another called out, "I've found some green treasure."

They were so happy. They put the shiny beads in their sacks and when they had finished digging, they said goodby to Mollie.

"The King will be very pleased with us," they said. "He will put all this treasure in a strong, safe box and turn the key. Goodby! Goodby!"

They marched off in a line, smiling and chattering. Mollie wondered what the King was like and if he wore a crown, but she never saw him. Perhaps she will, one day, if she is lucky.

Early in the Morning

Janet slept in a little room by herself. The window looked out on the garden. When she lay in bed, she could see the branches of a big cherry tree. In spring they were covered with white flowers. In summer they had green leaves and bunches of red cherries. In winter they were just bare brown.

One winter morning, as Janet lay in bed waiting for it to be time to get up, she thought she heard a little voice singing outside her window. It was a very little voice, but she could hear every word:

I am the Watchman of the Night,
My lantern gives a lovely light;
I'm here to put your troubles right.

I wonder who is singing outside, she thought.

The next morning, when it was still nearly dark, she heard the same little voice singing the same little song:

I am the Watchman of the Night,
My lantern gives a lovely light;
I'm here to put your troubles right.

It was such a pretty song that Janet sang it over to herself afterwards. Tomorrow I shall look out of the window and see who is there, she thought.

When tomorrow came, Janet heard the same voice singing the same song. She jumped out of bed and peeped between the curtains. The window was open and there, on the window-sill, was an elf. He was dressed in green with round, red buttons like cherries on his coat and a round, red pom-pom like a cherry on his hat. In his hand was a tiny lantern.

"Who are you?" asked Janet.

"I am the Watchman of the Night," said the elf. "All night long I go up and down the gardens and the fields and the woods, carrying my lantern and singing my song. I help anyone who is in trouble."

"Was anyone in trouble last night?" asked Janet.

"Yes. There was a spider who had fallen into a birdbath and could not get out. But I soon fished her out and took her back to her web. Goodby—perhaps we shall meet again."

The elf waved his hand and flew away into the cherry tree. Janet could hardly wait for the next morning to come. When she heard the little song she ran to the window and there was the Watchman with his tiny lantern.

"Was anyone in trouble last night?" she asked.

"Yes," said the elf. "A squirrel woke up because he was hungry and tried to find the nuts he had hidden in a hole, but he had forgotten where the hole was. I soon showed him the place and he had a good supper. Goodby—perhaps we shall meet again."

He waved his hand and flew away into the cherry tree.

The next morning Janet hoped very hard that the Watchman would come. She listened and listened and at last she heard his song and ran to the window.

"Please can you help *me*?" she asked. "I have a trouble to be put right."

"I'll do my best," said the Watchman. "What is wrong?"

"I've lost the key of my money-box and I want to unlock it today and take out some money. I want to buy Mother a birthday present. Oh, I've hunted everywhere!"

"It's in your handkerchief case," said the elf.

"But I've looked there," said Janet.

"Well, have another look. Shake out the handkerchiefs."

So Janet took out the case and shook the handkerchiefs, one by one, and sure enough, out fell the key.

"Thank you very, very much," said Janet. "Shall I see you tomorrow?"

"I must go to the fields for a time," said the Watchman. "The rabbits are always losing things and getting into trouble. They need a lot of help. But I shall be back when the cherries are ripe. The cherry tree is my home and that is why my buttons and my pom-pom are red like cherries and my coat green like cherry leaves."

"Goodby and thank you," said Janet.

"Goodby," said the elf and flew off, singing his little song:

> I am the Watchman of the Night,
> My lantern gives a lovely light;
> I'm here to put your troubles right.

Janet is waiting for the cherries to get red because she wants to see the kind little elf again. She hopes he will tell her all about the rabbits and the troubles they have been getting into. She often sings his song to herself.

The New Postman

Sometimes the animals and birds in the garden wanted to send letters to each other. They put these letters under a big stone, so they would not blow away or get wet. This was instead of dropping them in a mail-box.

But there was no postman to take the letters to the right people. If anyone was expecting a letter, he just looked under the stone to see if it was there waiting for him. This was rather awkward as letters sometimes lay there for weeks and weeks because no one had remembered to lift up the stone and have a look. Beetles nibbled the corners of the envelopes and snails left silvery marks all over the writing. The nice, neat, clean letters got all raggy and smudgy. No one could read what was written inside.

"We must have a postman," said the animals. "We must have a postman who can take the letters to the right people. Then they will be safe."

"Miaow! Miaow! Miaow! I think *I* should be a good postman," said the Kitten. "I can climb well, so I could take the letters up to creatures who live in trees. Do let me be the postman."

"Chatter! Chatter! Chatter!" said the Squirrel. "I should like to be the postman. When the ground is wet and muddy I can swing along from tree to tree and keep the letters dry and clean. I know all the quick ways from one part of the garden to another."

"Whuff! Whuff! Whuff!" said the Puppy. "What about me? I should be the best postman, I am sure. I am so used to carrying things about in my mouth. Why, I sometimes carry a bone around for a whole morning. I should never drop the letters."

The Robin did not say anything. He wanted to be a postman and fly from place to place with the letters in his beak, but the other animals sounded so clever and important. He did not feel at all clever and important. He just put his head on one side and listened and kept quiet.

"We can't have three postmen," said the Turtle. "That would be too many. Let Kitten and Squirrel and Puppy have a turn each and we can see who is the best. Kitten can be postman tomorrow. Squirrel can be postman the day after. Puppy can be postman the day after that."

The animals thought this was a very good idea. The next day Kitten had his turn. He had to take a letter to one of the hens in the hen-run. He set off very carefully, with the letter in his mouth. He walked along on his soft black paws with his fluffy tail straight up in the air and his

green eyes looking from side to side. When he got near the hen-run, a little, curly white feather blew by and tickled his nose. He sneezed: "A-tish-oo! A-tish-oo!" and forgot all about the letter. He jumped up to catch the tickly feather and the letter fell out of his mouth and blew away, up—up—up—over the hen-house—over the tree-tops—out of sight.

Kitten felt ashamed of himself. He drooped his fluffy tail and hung his head. He knew that no one would choose *him* to be the postman, now.

The next day it was Squirrel's turn. He had to take a letter to Owl, who lived in an oak tree. He held it safely between his white teeth and went swinging off from branch to branch. When he was almost there, a squirrel friend called from a beech tree:

"Stop a minute and taste one of my hazel nuts. They are fine and juicy."

"I mustn't stay long," said Squirrel, "but I just fancy a ripe nut." He laid the letter carefully on a branch and the two squirrels cracked themselves some nuts, "Crack! Crack! Crack!" and then gobbled them up, "Crunch! Crunch! Crunch!"

"I must go now," said Squirrel. "I am a postman today. Here is the letter I am taking to Owl." He turned to pick up the letter, but what had happened to it? The writing was smudged and the envelope was sopping wet. Squirrel had forgotten that it had rained in the night and the raindrops fell from the tree, drip—drip—drip—and spoiled the letter.

"Oh dear! Oh dear!" said Squirrel. "How terrible! Owl will not be pleased, I am sure, when I give him this untidy letter."

Owl was not at all pleased. Indeed, he was very cross. "You are a very stupid animal," he grumbled. "My beautiful letter is all wet. I can hardly read a word of it."

Squirrel went sadly home. He knew no one would choose *him* to be the postman.

The next day it was Puppy's turn. He had to take a letter to the fieldmice who lived in a bank at the end of the garden. He walked along slowly, the letter in his mouth. He was not going to let it blow away or get wet.

Presently he got to a patch of soil under a laurel bush where he always buried his bones. The soil was loose and rough because he was always scratching it up with his paws. As he looked, he felt he must have a nice scrabble in it. He quite forgot the thing in his mouth was a letter and not a bone and he quickly dug a lovely deep hole and BURIED it. Scratch! Scratch! Scratch! When he was covering the hole over, he remembered.

"What a terrible mistake I have made!" barked Puppy. "I must dig it up again at once." But the letter was spoiled. It was earthy and damp and crumpled.

Poor Puppy! How sad he felt. He knew no one would choose *him* to be the postman.

"We must find another postman," said Turtle and he looked around. Then he caught sight of Robin standing nearby, with his neat brown wings and cheerful breast. "Would you like to be a postman?" he asked.

"Yes, I would," said Robin.

So Robin had a turn. He had to take a letter to Mrs. Sparrow who lived under the roof. He flew straight there, holding the corner of the letter in his beak, and put it safely in the nest. He even stayed a little while to help Mrs. Sparrow read the difficult words.

"You must be our postman," said the Turtle, and all the other animals and birds agreed. Robin was very pleased and whistled with joy. He took letters everywhere, to creatures in trees and ditches and holes and nests, and never lost a single letter. He was a very good postman.

Old Mrs. Fieldmouse made him a little round, red postman's hat. He is very proud of it and always wears it. If you ever see a robin with a round, red hat to match his breast, you will know it is Robin the Postman.

The Silver Thimble

Have you ever played "Hunt the Thimble?" I'm sure you have. Everyone goes out of the room except one person who hides a thimble somewhere. Then he shouts, "Salt fish come to supper!" and everyone comes crowding in from the hall to look for the thimble.

This story is about a game of "Hunt the Thimble". A little girl called Sally had a party and the children wanted to play "Hunt the Thimble". Sally had the first turn because it was her birthday. When all the boys and girls were outside in the hall, and just Sally left behind, she shut the door and looked round for a good place. It was her own living-room so of course she knew the good places.

Should she put it behind a vase or under a chair? Should she try to reach the top of the bookcase or the TV? In the end she put it on one of the pedals under the piano.

Then Sally opened the door and called out, "Salt fish come to supper!" and everyone crowded in to search for the thimble. Some looked high. Some looked low. "Are we warm? Are we getting hot?" they asked. But no one was near the piano so no one was warm. Then, suddenly, Sally cried out, "The thimble's gone! It's disappeared! It isn't where I put it!"

Her mother looked under the piano and the children looked too and crept about on hands and knees over the floor. But there was no sign of the thimble.

"Oh, Mummy!" said Sally. "What shall we do? It was your best silver thimble with the tiny lion stamped inside."

"It must be somewhere," said her mother. "Don't let's worry. I'll find another thimble for you to play with instead."

Now behind the piano was a small, dark mouse-hole and in the small, dark mouse-hole lived a family of mice. The father mouse had seen the silver thimble shining and had darted out, quick as a flash, while Sally was opening the door, and had snatched it up and taken it into his hole. While the children were searching everywhere, he and his family were admiring the thimble.

"It is made of real silver," said Father Mouse, biting the edge. "I shall use it for my own special drinking cup."

"I think it would make a good plant pot," said Mother Mouse. "This is a dark hole and some flowers in a bright pot would cheer it up."

"It would make me a fine new hat," said the Girl

Mouse. "I should be proud to wear it."

"But I want it for myself," said the Boy Mouse. "It will make a drum and I shall beat it like this." He began hitting the thimble with a spoon. It sounded rather tinny.

By this time the mice were very angry with each other. They glared. They glowered. They growled. They lashed their tails and showed their teeth. They were cross all the evening and went to bed without saying goodnight to each other, all because of the silver thimble.

In the middle of the night, the mice woke up with a start. A tall, shining person with very long legs was standing outside their hole. "Snip-snap! Snip-snap!" said the tall shining person. "I am the scissors from the work-basket and I have come to get my thimble. Snip-snap! Give me my thimble or I will snip off your whiskers."

The mice were frightened and shivered and shook, but they did not want to give up their silver thimble.

Then a row of thin, pointed people with scratchy voices stood outside. "Scratch-scratch! Scratch-scratch!" said the pointed people. "We are the pins from the work-basket and we have come to get our thimble. Scratch-scratch! Give us our thimble or we will prick you."

The mice were more frightened and shivered and shook more than ever, but they did not want to give up their silver thimble.

Then a *very* sharp person with a long tail appeared. "Stitch-stitch! Stitch-stitch!" said the very sharp person. "I am the needle and thread from the work-basket and I have come to get my thimble. Stitch-stitch! Give me my thimble or I will sew up your hole and you will never be able to get out."

The mice did not want to be sewed up for ever and ever in their hole so they pushed the silver thimble out of the door and squeaked, "Take it!"

Then the scissors with shining legs and the pins with sharp points and the needle with a long tail took the thimble back to the work-basket where it belonged. The work-basket had a soft, padded lid, lined with silk, and was a very cozy place indeed, far cozier than a mouse-hole.

Sally's mother was very surprised to find her thimble there the next day. She was surprised, too, to see tiny teeth marks round the edge. But she never guessed they were where Father Mouse had bitten it to find out if it was real silver.

A Cradle for a Fairy

Sally lived in a house with a small yard. But it was large enough to play in. There was a piece of grass in the middle and an apple tree in one corner. A path ran all the way round the yard. Even when it had been raining and the grass was too wet to walk on, she could play on this little path.

One day, after tea, Sally was bouncing her ball on the path. Bounce—bounce—bounce—went the rubber ball. Bounce—bounce—bounce—BOUNCE! The last bounce was a very high one and the ball hit the apple tree and rolled away under some ferns.

As Sally stooped down to get it, she heard a sad little voice saying: "What shall I do? What shall I do? Oh dear, dear, what shall I do?"

Sally looked and listened. The sad little voice came from a brown spider who was sitting on one of the fern leaves. She had a white cross on her fat, round body which made her look like a bun with legs.

"What is the matter?" asked Sally. "Can I help you?"

"No, you can't help me. No one can help me," said the

spider. "I was spinning a cradle for the Fairy Queen's baby and it was nearly finished. Now your great bouncing ball has broken it. Oh, what shall I do?"

"I'm very sorry," said Sally. "Can't you spin another cradle?"

"I could, but I haven't time. A cradle takes me a whole day and the sun is setting now. It must be ready when the moon rises."

"What happens when the moon rises?" asked Sally.

"The Fairy Queen comes to dance in the moonlight with her friends. She likes to put her baby to sleep in a cobweb cradle. It is quiet and safe among the fern leaves and the baby can sleep while her mother dances on the moss at the foot of the apple tree."

"Don't be so sad," said Sally. "I think I can help you. Wait here while I run indoors to get something."

She ran indoors and came back with half a walnut shell. She put it down on the moss.

"Will this do for a cradle?"

The spider looked at it and felt it carefully with two of her eight legs. Then she shook her head.

"It is too rough for a fairy baby."

"But perhaps you have time to spin a cobweb blanket to put inside," said Sally. "Then it would be soft enough."

"So it would! So it would!" agreed the spider. "I'll start at once. It is a very good idea."

She set to work and spun a soft, fleecy, cobwebby blanket, just the right size. Sally spread it inside the half walnut shell and it covered all the rough part.

"*My* cradle was going to swing to and fro and hush the baby to sleep," said the spider. "Swinging cradles are the best for babies."

"But this one will rock," said Sally. "That is just as good." She touched the edge of the walnut shell with her finger and it rocked from side to side.

The spider was very pleased when she saw how well the

cradle rocked and how soft the blanket looked. She thanked Sally for her help.

Just then Sally's mother called: "Bedtime. Come along Sally," and Sally had to say goodnight to the spider and run indoors.

The next morning, Sally went down the garden path and looked carefully at the patch of moss at the foot of the apple tree. It looked exactly the same. Fairies are so tiny and their slippers are so small that they do not even flatten a carpet of moss.

Then Sally kneeled down and peeped under the fern leaves and saw the walnut shell cradle. The cobweb blanket was lying inside, a little crumpled because it had been wrapped round a fairy baby.

"I do hope the baby was good and did not cry," thought Sally. "I wish I had seen her asleep, while her mother danced in the moonlight."

Little Wife Goody

There was once a little boy named Ben who lived by the sea. When he looked out of his bedroom window, he could see a smooth, sandy beach with the waves breaking in curving ripples. When he lay awake in bed, early in the morning, he could hear the lap-lap of the water and the cries of the seagulls.

Ben had never played in a park, and the cottage where he lived had a very tiny yard. The beach was his playing place. He had only to open the front door, run across a rough, sandy track, down some stone steps, and he was on the sea shore. If his mother wanted him, she just called, "Ben! Ben!" and he heard and ran home.

His favorite toys were his spade and pail, and his green shrimping net. Sometimes he caught a few shrimps. Sometimes he caught a crab. Sometimes he caught only seaweed. Whatever it was, he looked at it carefully, and then threw it back into the sea, where it belonged.

Ben had a big sister named Martha, with two long brown braids hanging over her shoulders. When she was not at school, she often played with him and told him stories. There was a low stone wall between the sandy track and the beach, and Martha and Ben used to lean on the wall and look out to sea. Far away, over the sea, they could see another beach with golden sand.

"It is just like your beach, really," said their mother. "Children play on it just as you play here." But Martha and Ben pretended it was quite different. They called it The Lucky Land, and made up stories about it.

"Everyone has strawberry jam for tea in The Lucky Land," Ben would say.

"No one gets tangles in their hair," added Martha, shaking her two long braids, "and they don't have to make their beds."

"And boys don't need to wash. They just stay dirty."

"And girls have lots of pockets—big ones—four in every dress."

One morning, the postman came along the sandy path and knocked on the door of Ben's cottage, and Ben ran to open it.

"This is for you," said the postman, giving him a small, square parcel.

"Thank you," said Ben, jumping up and down with excitement. "It is from granny. I know her nice curly B's. No one does such curly B's as granny." Although Ben could not read yet, he knew how to write his own name.

He undid the string, took off the brown paper, and underneath was a piece of white paper. He took that off, and underneath was some soft tissue paper. Inside the soft tissue paper was a tiny wooden figure, like a tiny wooden doll. It was an old woman with a blue shawl over her head, and a yellow blouse, and a striped skirt. Her clothes were only painted on. She was shaped rather like an acorn, but flat at the bottom, so that she could stand. She was so small that she fitted inside Ben's hand.

"I shall call her Little Wife Goody," said Ben, looking at her rosy cheeks and her smile. Then he noticed a crack round her middle, where her waist was. He held her tightly, gripped her head, and twisted it round. Yes, it turned a little, and then a little more, and a little more, till

she had come right in half. He held her top half in one hand and her bottom half in the other. She was hollow inside and in the hollow was a little red ball.

Ben took out the little red ball and looked at it carefully, but it was too tiny to unscrew.

"It must be Little Wife Goody's heart," he said, and he put it back inside her and screwed her two halves together again.

Ben liked Little Wife Goody very much, from the first moment he saw her. She was so bright and smiling and such a comfortable size for carrying about. He never went anywhere without her. Sometimes she was inside his hand, safe and warm. Sometimes she was inside his pocket. At meal times she sat on the table beside his plate. At night she slept under his pillow.

Martha liked Little Wife Goody as well. When Ben let her slip down the crack of the arm chair, down, down, where his fingers could not reach, Martha poked and prodded till she felt Little Wife Goody's head, and caught hold of it, and pulled her up to safety.

"We'll make some magic," said Martha. "Then she may not get lost again. Come with me and I'll show you how to do it."

First they went into the little yard.

"Roll her three times in the soil," said Martha, "and then nothing on earth can hurt her." So Ben rolled Little Wife Goody three times in the soil.

"Now dip her three times in water so nothing in the water can hurt her." So Ben put some water in a bowl and dipped Little Wife Goody three times.

"Now wave her three times in the air so nothing in the air can hurt her." So Ben waved Little Wife Goody three times in the air.

He felt very pleased that he had made magic. He hoped dear Little Wife Goody would always be safe, on land, or water, or in the air.

Little Wife Goody had a very happy life with Ben. No wonder she smiled all the time. He made her gardens on the beach, with shells round the edge and seaweed for flowers. He made sand-castles with tunnels through them, and put her on the top. He dug holes so deep that the water rose and filled them like a lake, and he floated a boat on the lake, with her on board.

One day, when the tide was high and the waves covered the beach, Ben was leaning on the wall looking over the sea to The Lucky Land. The sun was shining and the sand was golden, it was so bright that he had to crinkle up his eyes under his sun hat. He held Little Wife Goody on the wall so she could look at The Lucky Land as well. The waves were breaking at the foot of the wall—splash! splash! splash! The spray was cold and wet on his face.

Suddenly, Ben never knew how, Little Wife Goody slipped off the wall and fell down, down, down, into the water. The tide had just turned, and a great wave curled over and flung her away from the wall. Her little blue

head bobbed for a minute, and then another wave broke and carried her further away. And another. And another. And another.

"Oh dear!" cried Ben. "She's gone. She's drowned. Oh, what shall I do? Martha! Martha! Hurry—M-A-R-T-H-A!"

Martha came running out of the cottage and stood beside him. They both watched the little blue head bobbing up and down, up and down, among the waves.

"She won't drown," said Martha. "See how well she swims. Remember the magic you made to keep her safe in water."

"But I made the magic with water from the tap, not salt water," said Ben miserably.

"I'll get daddy's telescope and we'll look through that," said Martha, running indoors.

By now, Little Wife Goody was only a speck. Ben tried to look through the telescope, but it was not much good. The sea was so big, and Little Wife Goody was so small. Tears kept coming into his eyes and making everything look blurred and misty.

Martha took the telescope and watched a little longer.

"She's still swimming. She's a wonderful swimmer. A seagull has just flown over her."

Soon, even the tiny blue speck that was Little Wife

Goody's head had floated out of sight. There were only the waves to watch, tossing the white foam like white horses tossing their manes.

Ben stayed by the wall till it was dinner time. Mother had poached him an egg in a nest of mashed potato but it was difficult to swallow. He did miss Little Wife Goody, standing by his plate, smiling. Afterwards, Martha read him a story and mother took him to the village in the bus but he did not feel much better. He wished he had Little Wife Goody in his hand instead of his bus ticket. She was such a smooth comfortable shape for holding. Just the right size.

When bed time came, Ben could not get to sleep. He turned his pillow over to find a cool place, and he heard the clock downstairs strike eight. He wondered where Little Wife Goody was sleeping. Was she still swimming in the water, bobbing up and down among the waves?

Just when he had decided that he never would get to sleep and he would have to stay awake till morning, Martha came in. She was wearing her bathrobe, and her long braids swung like two ropes as she sat on his bed and leaned over him.

"Ben," she whispered, "I've heard from Little Wife Goody. She's quite safe."

Ben sat straight up. "Where is she?"

"She has landed in The Lucky Land. It was a long

journey over the sea, up and down among the waves, but at last, a wave washed her safely on to the shore."

"How do you know?" asked Ben.

"A seagull brought me the news. When she found herself on the beach, she sat on a rock to get dry, and while she was resting and getting dry, dozens of little wooden people, just like herself, came from holes in the rocks and under the seaweed. Big ones and small ones. Talking ones and quiet ones. Children and babies. They all said, 'Welcome, Little Wife Goody. Welcome to The Lucky Land'."

"Is she happy away from me?"

"Well, she isn't exactly happy, because she likes you best. She says she always will. But the little wooden people are very kind to her. She says, 'Goodnight. Sleep tight'."

While Ben was thinking about Little Wife Goody and The Lucky Land, he fell fast asleep. Martha tiptoed away and put her bedroom slipper in the door to keep it from closing, so she could hear if Ben called. But Ben did not call. He slept till morning.

The next day Martha and Ben took a picnic to a cave in another part of the beach. They collected seaweed and made a seaweed garden, and Ben forgot about Little Wife Goody for quite a long time. But when they got home and he went to bed, he wished she was under his pillow where he could touch her. Martha came in to say good-night.

"Any more news?" asked Ben.

"Yes. The Lucky Land people like Little Wife Goody so much that they want her to be their queen. They have made her a shell crown. She is very busy looking after people who are not well, and hushing babies who cry, and teaching the children to play 'hunt the thimble' with a pebble."

"Does she wish I was there with her?"

"Yes, she does. Always. She looks over the sea to your beach and wonders what you are doing."

Every evening, Martha gave Ben news of Little Wife Goody. She was a kind queen. She taught the little wooden people to sing and make seaweed gardens. They had never heard of cereal for breakfast, or pancakes with syrup, so she had to do a lot of cooking.

One evening, Martha said, "The seagull cannot come for a little while. He has to help his wife to build a nest. But Little Wife Goody says she is sending you a friend to keep you company. Look on the beach tomorrow at nine o'clock and you will find him."

Next morning Ben could hardly wait till the clock had struck nine. He ran out of the door, over the sandy path, and down the steps to the beach. He ran here, there, everywhere, searching among the seaweed and the stones. Soon he saw a parcel with a label tied on. The label said: TO BEN FROM LITTLE WIFE GOODY. He opened the parcel and inside was a little wooden clown.

The clown was the same size as Little Wife Goody, like a big acorn, and he came in half round the middle just like

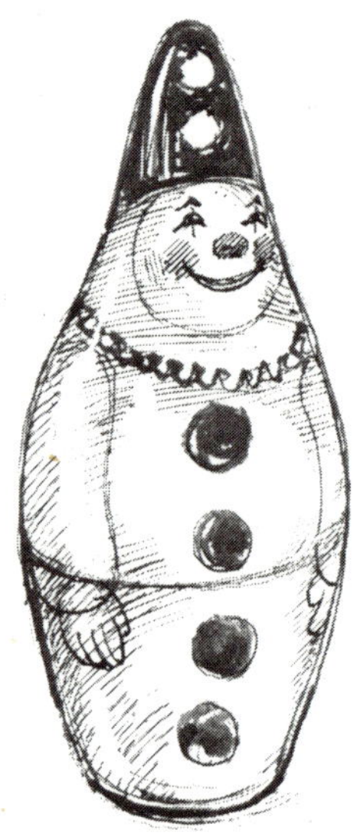

her. And he had a red heart inside, too. He wore a pointed clown's hat, and had dabs of red on his cheeks and on his nose, like a real clown. And red pompoms on his hat and on his shirt. Of course, all these clothes were painted on.

As for his face, it was smiling, a great, wide, happy, ear-to-ear smile. Ben just had to smile back.

"I shall call my clown Smiling Sam," he said, "and I shall take him everywhere with me."

So Smiling Sam went everywhere with Ben. He went on the beach. He sat on the table at meal times. He slept under Ben's pillow at night.

When Martha came to say goodnight, she asked Ben, "What has Smiling Sam been doing today?" and Ben told her, "He has been sailing in my boat," or "He has been building a sand-castle with six windows," or "He has been collecting oyster shells."

When the tide is really high and the waves break against the sea wall, Ben puts Smiling Sam safely in his pocket. He looks across the water to the shore of The Lucky Land, and he wonders what Little Wife Goody is doing. But he cannot quite remember what Little Wife Goody looks like. So he brings Smiling Sam out of his pocket and looks at him instead. He is always smiling, from ear to ear. He even smiles when he is asleep, so he must have happy dreams.

The Cottage by the Sea

I

Once upon a time there were three children who lived in a little village by the sea. Their cottage had whitewashed walls, a brown roof, and a curl of smoke coming from the chimney. The children were named Jenny, and Emma, and William. Jenny was the oldest. She was ten, Emma was eight, and little William was six.

When the children looked out of the window of their living-room, they could see the sandy beach curved like a new moon, and a small, stone jetty or pier stretching out like a long arm into the sea. The stones of the jetty were rough and uneven, but the children's bare feet were so tough and hard that they could run and jump on them as easily as on soft grass.

Here and there among the stones were heavy, iron rings where the fishermen could tie up their boats. Their father tied his boat to one of these rings. It was an old boat with patched sails but he was very proud of it.

The children's mother was usually very busy, cooking and washing and mending. Whenever the children went out to play, she always said, "Don't go where you can't see the smoke from our chimney." So they played on the beach or on the cliffs behind the cottage but never went so far that they could not see the curl of smoke. Then their mother knew they were safe.

One Saturday in summer, their mother said, "You are getting big now, and sensible as well. You can go further away if you wish, along the cliff top. I will give you some lunch to take with you, but you must be home before the sun sets."

The children promised not to stay out too late. They put their food in a satchel, and Jenny, because she was the oldest, slipped it over her shoulder.

"Goodby, Mother!" they called, "Goodby! We'll be very careful and good."

The three children followed the little winding cliff path, among the green leaves of the wild shrubs. They were so hardy that even William did not care when his bare legs became scratched with the prickles. On and on along the path they went, sometimes stopping to look over the edge of the cliff, down to the sea below. They saw lovely sandy beaches and great, black rocks bearded with green seaweed. A seagull flew right past their faces and they could

see his pink feet tucked underneath him.

"I hope we aren't lost," said Emma, who was not very brave. "Shall we go back now?"

"Of course we're not lost," said Jenny. "There is only this one path and it will lead us straight home when we are tired."

Suddenly little William stopped and called to the others to come and stand beside him. They ran to him and looked down, down, over the cliff's edge. There, on the beach below, was an old cottage. It was a tumbledown place, not fit for anyone to live in, with shingles missing from the roof, and bracken and nettles growing as high as the windows. But it must have been a pretty little house once, so snug and sheltered against the cliff.

"Let's go and explore," said Jenny. "I see a path leading down the cliff. Take my hand William, and you'll be all right." They went down the steep little path and soon reached the cottage.

First they walked around the outside. They did not say a word, the cottage looked so sad and lonely. The door had rotted away and there was no glass in the windows. It was very quiet, with only the waves lapping on the shore and a seagull crying overhead.

After a time they were used to the silence and the strangeness, and William went to the door and stepped

inside the front room. The other two followed.

This room was draughty, and there were ferns and toad-stools growing out of the floor. But there was another room beyond, and that was more comfortable.

"Look! Look!" cried William. "Just look here!"

They crowded into the next room after him and saw, in the fireplace, the remains of a fire. Nearby was a pile of driftwood, neatly stacked. Against the wall was a bed of piled-up bracken leaves.

"Someone lives here," whispered Emma. "Someone sleeps here. I wonder whoever it could be!"

Jenny stooped and put her hand into the ashes in the fireplace. "They are still warm," she said. "Someone must have cooked his breakfast here this morning."

The children tried to imagine who could want to live in such a place. A tramp, perhaps. A gypsy. Someone very poor who had no money to pay for a proper bed.

They tiptoed out into the sunshine and ate their lunch sitting on a rock. Their mother had given them thick, thick slices of bread, chunks of cheese, three wedges of gingerbread, three rosy apples, and a bag of of hard candy.

"Shall we leave something in the little cottage for the person who sleeps there?" suggested Jenny. "I can spare my apple. And a piece of candy," she added after a pause.

"So can I," said Emma.

"I suppose I can, too," said William, who wanted to eat his apple himself but did not like to seem greedy. So they put the three apples and the three pieces of candy on the bracken bed.

Then Emma picked a bunch of sea pinks that were growing in the sand outside the cottage. She arranged them and put damp moss round the stalks to keep them fresh. William added a few bits of driftwood to the neat pile to help the person who lived in the cottage to make his fire. Then they scrambled up the steep path and turned back towards home. They reached their door just as the sun was setting, and their mother was putting potatoes on to boil.

During the next few days, the children often thought about the deserted cottage. If there was a strong wind, they wondered how the stranger who slept there kept warm. How the wind would whistle through the chinks in the walls and the holes in the roof! If the night was calm and mild, they were glad. The bracken bed would be quite comfortable on such a night.

The next Saturday was sunny and the children asked their mother to pack up another picnic for them. So she filled the satchel with good things to eat, and they set off along the cliff path. They had the whole day ahead of them, hours and hours, but they could not help hurrying. Jenny strode on so quickly that Emma got out of breath, keeping up with her. As for William, he had to trot very fast on his short legs. But he did not mind. He was longing to see the little cottage again and to find out if the apples and the candy were gone. If they were still there, he decided to eat his straight away, even if the sour ball had gone soft and was sticking to the paper.

It did not seem long before they reached the steep cliff

path, and went sliding and slithering down from the cliff top on to the beach. They ran to the door of the cottage, and then drew back. Suppose someone were inside? They did not want to burst in and disturb him. It was very quiet standing there, with the waves gently breaking, and the ivy flapping in the breeze.

"Is there anyone at home!" called Jenny softly. Her voice echoed queerly, but there was no answer, only a seagull crying.

"Let's go in," whispered William. "I'll go, if you'll come too." He tiptoed into the first room and then through to the second room. Jenny and Emma were close behind him. Somehow, after one glance, they knew the room was quite deserted. The ashes had blown about the floor. There was no pile of driftwood. The fireplace felt cold when they knelt down to feel it with their hands.

"He has gone away," said Jenny.

"And our apples and candy have gone, too," added William. "I expect he enjoyed them. He must have wondered who put them on his bed."

"But he has left something else behind," said Emma. "Look! On this stone in the corner! And there's a piece of paper with writing on it."

The writing was very smudged and thick, as if it had been done with the end of a burnt stick. It just said:

THANK YOU.

Beside the paper were three objects which made the children gasp with delight. There was a whistle carved from a piece of wood, a polished, black tooth of a shark, and a necklace of fan-shaped shells.

"One each!" said Emma. "What a kind, clever man!" There was no arguing or quarreling, because the presents just suited the children perfectly.

William reached for the whistle as Emma stretched out her hand for the shark's tooth. Jenny tied the necklace of shells round her neck.

They ate their picnic, every bit this time, and played round the cottage till it was time to go home. They mended some of the holes with stones, and packed the cracks with moss to keep out the wind. The cottage did not seem strange any longer. Just old.

II

Jenny, and Emma, and William often visited the old cottage on the beach, and played there. They did not forget the person who once slept in the cottage, and they took care of the presents he left behind.

One day, Jenny said to their mother, "Do come and see our little cottage. Come today."

"Yes, please come," went on Emma.

"It isn't too far for you," added William kindly. "My legs hardly ache at all, now I know the way."

"Very well," said their mother. "You go off now, and I'll come later, when I am ready. I will bring the picnic with me."

The children rushed away. When they reached the cottage, they took off their jerseys, as they were hot, and hung them on a stick wedged beside the door. This made the cottage look like home.

"I'm going to make a surprise for Mother," said Jenny.

"So am I," said Emma. "A really good one."

"And so am I," added William. "I won't even tell you what it is going to be. Anyhow, I can't tell you. I don't know myself yet!"

Jenny found a flat slate that had fallen from the roof, and she propped it up on four stones to make a table. On the table she put round oyster shells for plates, and small, curly ones, like snail shells, for cups. She found a few blackberries for each plate, growing on the side of the cliff, and she put rosettes and ribbons of seaweed here and there to look pretty. Then she floated yellow gorse flowers in a big, deep shell in the middle of the table.

Emma wrote MOTHER in the sand with a stick, and then filled in the letters with pebbles.

Little William was busy with something very secret. "Go away!" he shouted, if Jenny or Emma came near, "Go away!"

Mother arrived at the right moment, when the surprises were ready. She called to them from the top of the cliff, and William scrambled up the path to take her hand, and help her down.

First mother looked at Jenny's surprise. "I wish I was small enough to sit at that dear little table," she said. "May I eat one of the blackberries?"

Then she admired her name written in pebbles. "I did not know Emma could write so well. What a big, beautiful M!"

Now it was William's turn. "Come with me," he whispered. "Come with me to my surprise."

They all followed him. He had dug a deep hole in a bank of sand. "That is my oven," he explained. "I'm a baker. Here are my buns." He showed them four white stones on a slate. "Now I am going to bake them in my hot oven." He wrapped a handkerchief round his hand, as if the slate were too hot to hold, and pushed the buns into the oven.

"They're ready now," he said after a pause. "They're nicely done, I'm sure. What a lovely smell!"

He put his hand into the oven and fumbled about inside, making clinking noises. Then he pulled out the slate and there were four BROWN stones on it, instead of white.

"See, my buns are brown!" he cried, jumping up and down. "My hot oven has cooked them. What do you think of that?"

"I think it is wonderful," said mother. "What a good baker you are! Not one is burnt!"

Then it was mother's turn to give the children a surprise. Besides sandwiches and apples for the picnic, she had brought three little cookie men, one each. They had raisins for eyes and nose, a cherry for a mouth, and a row of raisin buttons for the jacket.

The children nibbled an arm or a leg first, whichever took their fancy, and then a bite of hat, till there was no cookie man left.

After they had shown their mother the cottage, and played a little longer, it was time to go home. Jenny and Emma led the way, jumping over the prickly weeds. William, tired but happy, walked with mother, holding her hand, and sometimes blowing his whistle.

The Robber

One morning, Hedgehog was scampering round the garden, his bristles shining in the sun, when he met his best friend Turtle. Turtle was often very lively at this hour, walking briskly along, his eyes bright and his flat head turning from side to side. But, today, he was sitting quite still, in one spot.

"You look very sad," remarked Hedgehog.

"It's unfair!" muttered Turtle, his head half hidden in the folds of his neck. "It's a shame! It's a disgrace!"

"What is unfair?" asked Hedgehog.

"Food is unfair. Or rather my food is. I shall soon starve to death. When they find my dead body under the rhubarb leaves, they'll be sorry!"

"What do you mean? Do, please, explain." Hedgehog wrinkled his little brown face into a frown. What he could see of Turtle looked quite ordinary. Four stout, short legs. Tail as usual. Face as plump as ever, in spite of cross expression. But, of course, most of Turtle was hidden under his hard shell. Perhaps he was shrinking under there, shrinking slowly, fading away out of sight.

"Everyone else has as much food as he or she can eat, and the right kind, too," went on Turtle. "Owl catches as many mice as he can swallow. Dandy the dog is always burying bones he cannot finish. Winko the kitten has milk on his whiskers whenever I see him. And what did *you* find to eat last night for supper? Tell me that!"

"I don't remember exactly. A dozen or so worms, slugs and beetles, a snail or two, a few odds and ends by way of pudding, a couple of frogs, I believe."

"A square meal! A positive feast! And where is *my* square meal? Where is *my* feast? Tell me that!"

Hedgehog shook his head. He did not know. Turtle went on. "Under wire netting, that's where it is. Under wire netting, safely fixed by the gardener to keep me out."

"Yes. I saw him putting the lettuce bed into a kind of cage of wire netting. But this garden is full of things for you to eat. You are always chewing dandelions and yellow pansies and tender shoots."

"Those are only extras. Mere titbits. Lettuce is my proper food. Crisp, young lettuce. Young, green, curly, crumpled little hearts that melt in the mouth."

Hedgehog felt very sorry for his friend. He would gladly have brought him a few juicy worms or a fat slug but Turtle ate only green things.

"Let's ask Owl," he suggested cheerfully. "Owl will know what to do. He is so wise. Come along, now. We may just catch him before he goes to sleep after his night's hunting."

They scurried off, Hedgehog running ahead and Turtle following at a fine speed, considering he was about to die of starvation.

Owl had just tidied his hole in the hollow oak for the night, and preened his feathers. He was feeling drowsy, but he listened to Turtle's sad tale without actually falling asleep in the middle.

"Grow lettuce yourself," he advised, yawning and nodding.

"Where can I get the seed?"

"Shelf in the tool-shed."

"Where shall I plant them?"

"Anywhere."

"But I can't read what it says on the seed packets."

This time there was no answer, only a snore. Owl was asleep.

Turtle and Hedgehog hurried to the tool-shed. They could not reach the high shelf themselves where the seeds were kept, but young Twig Squirrel climbed up and brought them down. Luckily there was a picture of each plant on the outside of the packet, so there was no need to worry over the writing.

Turtle was tempted to grow radishes when he saw the round, rosy ones in the picture. How good they would be to crunch, but perhaps a little hard. He turned to the next packet.

This showed neat rows of peas, each pod ready to burst open. But the pods were rather high and he was a short kind of animal. He pondered over beans. Cabbages. Carrots. Then he gazed at gay pictures of pinks and corn-

flowers. But when Twig Squirrel handed him a packet of lettuce seeds, he forgot everything else. The picture showed an enormous lettuce. A giant lettuce. Almost all heart and no outside to speak of.

Twig put the other packets back on the shelf and Turtle went off with the lettuce packet in his mouth. He planned to meet Twig and Hedgehog that evening and make a seed bed. He spent the day looking at the packet and planning where he would take his first bite—right in the very middle of the curly heart!

When evening came, and the gardener had gone home, and Teddy and Susan, who played in the garden, were in bed, Turtle met his friends among the raspberries. Dandy and Winko came as well, and several mice and squirrels.

"We must choose a very secret place for my seed bed," said Turtle, "where we shall not be disturbed."

"What about the patch by the pond?"

"That's far too open. Everyone will see us."

"Or the bit near the holly bush?"

"That's too shadowy. Nothing will grow."

Almost every inch of the garden was suggested in turn and someone found something wrong with it.

"Let me flip a nutshell into the air," said Twig Squirrel, "while you all cross your paws for luck. Where it falls we will have the seed bed."

"We can try," agreed Turtle, doubtfully, "but I can't cross my paws. They aren't arranged that way."

Twig quickly found an old nutshell and gave it a sharp flick. Up in the air it went—over the lilac—and down in a sheltered corner between the summer-house and the hedge. Everyone gave a sigh of relief, and paws were uncrossed. They set to work at once.

The seed bed, when finished, would have pleased a real gardener. So many claws and paws had scratched and raked it over that the soil was as fine and soft as sand. Then Turtle, trembling with excitement, bit off the corner of the packet, and slowly crept up and down, letting the seed fall out in a thin line. Hedgehog followed, covering the seed lightly, while Dandy brought a can of water from the pond in his mouth and watered the bed well.

Tired but happy, Turtle crept away to his bedroom under the rhubarb leaves, and dreamed of giant lettuces, rows and rows of them, all his own.

Turtle spent most of his time in his new garden, making sure that no robber bird stole a single seed. In a week, the first green shoots appeared. Here Owl came in useful. He had once read a gardening book and remembered some of the hints. He gave good advice to Turtle and his helpers.

"Water well," he said, and they watered well.

"Thin out the seedlings," and they thinned out the seedlings.

"Hoe! Transplant! Weed! Thin again!" As these wise words came from the hollow oak, they were acted on at once. The little garden would have taken first prize in a competition. Not a weed. Not a stone. Not a drooping plant. Only fine, young lettuce, evenly spaced out.

They were not, it is true, *quite* as large and juicy as the ones in the picture on the packet but each grew a tight little heart, and, at last, Turtle said that the very next day he intended to eat one for breakfast.

Early in the morning, Turtle went to his garden to choose the first lettuce. The hedge smelled sweet with the dew still on it, and the sun shone warmly. His cry of horror, when he saw what had happened during the

night, brought Hedgehog and Twig and the others quickly to his side. Then their cries were joined with his. Every lettuce had a nibble taken out of its heart. Not one had escaped. Some robber had tasted each in turn.

Turtle almost wept with rage and despair. Dandy howled. Winko mewed. Hedgehog growled. The squirrels wrung their paws and the mice squeaked.

"It's only a very tiny nibble," said Dandy at last.

"The lettuces aren't exactly spoiled."

"But they *are* spoiled," raged Turtle. "Quite, quite spoiled. Do you think I am going to eat other people's leavings? Not I! I shall keep watch tonight, and if the robber comes again, I'll give him what he deserves."

"I'll watch with you," offered several animals, but Turtle refused their help.

"No, thank you. I shall keep watch alone. I can deal with him single-handed. I'll bite his nose! I'll scratch out his eyes! I'll tear his ears off! I'll make his fur fly!"

As Turtle was the most gentle and timid of creatures, these threats sounded specially horrible.

"I'll jag him into a jig-saw!" went on Turtle. "I'll rip him into ribbons!" The others felt almost sorry for the robber, wicked though he was. Did he really deserve to have all these terrible things done to him?

That night, Turtle hid under the hedge, and dozed lightly till the first cock crowed. There were all the usual early morning sounds. Birds stirring in their nests. Drowsy chirpings. A distant train. But when would that other sound begin? Stealthy feet, perhaps creeping, perhaps scampering. His nose sniffed the air for a strange smell.

Suddenly he lifted his head. The robber was coming, nearer, and nearer. There was a scratching of dry soil as someone pressed through the hedge. In a few seconds Turtle would be able to see him, face to face.

The robber walked quite openly into view, looking about boldly, not trying to hide. Why did not Turtle attack him? Bite him and scratch him? Jag him into a jig-saw? Make his fur fly?

To begin with, there was no fur to fly. The robber was mostly shell and scaly skin. No wonder Turtle opened his eyes very wide with surprise when he saw, in front of him, an elegant and charming lady turtle. He came from his hiding place, unable to say a word.

"Good morning, Sir," said the lady turtle. "Are you the owner of this delightful lettuce garden? I have never seen a more beautiful one, not in all my travels, and I may say that I have lived in many strange places."

"Yes, it's mine," answered Turtle gruffly. "It's mine all right."

"How very kind of you to allow me to feast off your home-grown salad. Remarkably kind! Especially as we have not been introduced. My name is Princess Dido and I come from Greece."

"They just call me Turtle."

"A plain, noble name. Will you let me pay for what I have already eaten? A bunch of dandelions, perhaps, or a few young radishes?"

"Certainly not," protested Turtle. "Eat all you want, when you want. I feel ready for breakfast myself. Will you join me as my guest?"

Princess Dido was willing and the pair of them ate together, a nibble here and there, talking between mouthfuls.

"I came from the land of Greece in a barrel," said Princess Dido, "with dozens and dozens of my relations. Some men grabbed us from the peaceful rocks, where we were basking in the sun, and packed us in so tightly that we could hardly breathe. Then they nailed the lid on the barrel. Oh, how we longed for water and fresh food! Many of us died. The little ones, no bigger than crab-apples, died first. But I lived through the long voyage, perhaps because I was pressed against a crack in the side of the barrel. I could get a taste of sea air.

"I was taken to a shop, and the people who bought me were kind. But I missed my freedom. I was used to rocks, and the smell of wild thyme, and the company of my brothers and sisters. They bored a hole in my shell, threaded a string through, and tied me to a post, so I was a prisoner. But I bit through the string and escaped, and, after a long and weary journey, I found my way to your quiet garden."

Turtle was shocked to see the hole in the Princess's

shell. What could be worse than not being able to go where one wanted? Turtle described the garden, and the animals and birds who lived there. He suggested that the Princess should pay him a long visit, and meet all his friends. She accepted the invitation, gladly.

In the meantime, Hedgehog, and Twig Squirrel, and the others had tiptoed near to see what was happening. They expected to find a horrid scene. Blood splashed everywhere. Fur flying. Probably a dead body among the lettuce. All they saw, however, was Turtle and a small, charming companion, very like himself but lighter in color, strolling up and down, eating and chatting.

Owl looked down upon them from the roof of the summer-house. He was never surprised at anything, and only remarked, "Two's company. Three's none," and flew off to his oak tree. He had had a good night's hunting, and wanted to go to sleep.

The other animals stole away as Turtle offered Princess Dido a juicy lettuce heart, saying in a happy voice, "I used to feel lonely before you came. Now I shall have a companion. There are so many things I want to tell you that only another turtle could understand."

"Of course," answered the Princess, taking the lettuce heart with a smile. "I, too, have much to tell. Now when I lived in Greece . . ."

An Old Gentleman in a Fur Coat

Tammy and Lulu were brother and sister. They lived in the forest. They were allowed to play in the garden by the house, which their father had made. It was fenced round with wooden posts and in one place there was a gate. The garden was very tidy. There were flower beds and patches of vegetables and a narrow path. There was a swing for Tammy and Lulu to swing on. There was a little round pond like a mirror.

Tammy and Lulu liked playing in the tidy garden and swinging on the swing, but they longed to explore the forest beyond the fence. The forest was wild and untidy. Ferns and creepers and flowers and bushes grew in a tangle together and up above were the branches of the tall trees.

Sometimes a bird with bright feathers flew among the trees, giving a harsh, unfriendly cry. Sometimes a monkey swung nimbly from branch to branch. Sometimes, especially at night, they heard the roar of wild animals.

"Father, please may we play in the forest?" pleaded the children.

"You are ungrateful," said their father, "I have made you a safe, pretty garden to play in and you are not contented. What more do you want?"

"We want to explore," they said. "We want to see the strange birds and strange animals and strange flowers."

"The forest is full of dangers," said their father. "There are wild animals with sharp teeth and strong claws who would eat you up in a jiffy. When you hear them roaring at night, they are roaring with hunger."

"We are very small," said Lulu. "We are hardly worth eating."

"And we are very thin," added Tammy. "You often say what thin legs we have."

"No one would want us for dinner."

"Stop this foolish talk," said their father sternly, "and be content to play inside the safe fence I have made for you."

But Tammy and Lulu could not stop thinking about the forest and one day, when their father was out and their mother was busy, they slipped through the gate and closed it quietly behind them. They found they could not run along as easily as they did on the garden path. They had to push their way through bushes and branches. But they did not mind as there was so much that was different to hear and see and smell.

A hot gust of wind blew in their faces.

"I smell spiced cake," said Tammy.

"I smell strawberries," said Lulu.

"And I smell damp clothes drying."

"And I smell wet leaves."

They went on together, delighted by the scarlet and purple butterflies, and the green lizards that flicked out of sight like the flick of a whip. Soon they came to a clearing where the sun shone warmly on the ground. Here they met someone very large and fat, dressed in brown fur.

"G-r-r!" said the person.

"Good morning, Sir," said Tammy and Lulu.

"G-r-r!" said the person again. "Why don't you run away? I am a bear and bears eat people."

"Why should I run away from an old gentleman in a fur coat?" asked Tammy.

"And an old gentleman with a bad cold," went on Lulu. "You sound hoarse as if your throat were sore."

"But I DO eat people!" and the bear opened his mouth and showed a red tongue and two rows of sharp white teeth.

"Well, it wouldn't be any use eating us. We are so thin and small that we're not worth the trouble. Goodby, Sir."

"Goodby," said Lulu, "and take care of your cold."

Tammy and Lulu went on through the forest and the bear sat down on a tree stump and looked puzzled.

"Well, I never did in all my born days!" he growled to himself.

After a while the children met another large person dressed in stripes.

"P-s-s-t!" said the large person, spitting and arching his back.

"Good morning, Sir," said Tammy and Lulu.

"P-s-s-t!" spat the person again. "Why don't you run away? I am a tiger and tigers eat people."

"Why should I run away from a striped cat?" asked Tammy.

"A striped cat like our Mitzi at home, only bigger," went on Lulu. "Your eyes are the same and so are your whiskers and the way you lash your tail from side to side."

"But I DO eat people," said the tiger, and he opened his mouth and showed two rows of pointed white teeth and a narrow pink tongue.

"Just like Mitzi's, only bigger," said Lulu. "Goodby, Sir!"

"Goodby," said Tammy.

The children went on through the forest and the tiger lay down in the shade and looked puzzled.

"Well, I never did in all my born days," he said to himself.

After a while the children were walking along a narrow path when they found their way blocked by a very prickly person.

"Snitch! Snitch!" squeaked the prickly person.

"Good morning, Sir," said Tammy and Lulu.

"Snitch! Snitch!" squeaked the person again. "Why don't you run away? I am a porcupine and if you touch me I shall prick you with my sharp needles. Even the lion, the king of the forest, dare not come near. He is frightened of my prickles."

"You are only a pincushion," said Lulu, "like the pincushion my mother has in her work-basket, only much bigger. And hers is prettier because it is made of red velvet."

"You are not even a polite pincushion," said Tammy, "or you would move to one side and let us pass. There is room for us all. But as you are, perhaps, very old and feeble, we will let you pass instead," and he and Lulu pressed their way through the undergrowth and got by without brushing a prickle on the porcupine.

They went on their way through the forest and the porcupine put out his head as far as it would go and watched them, looking puzzled.

"Old indeed! Feeble indeed!" he said to himself. "Well, I never did in all my born days!"

After a while the children found that the path led them beside a slow, muddy stream with rushes growing at the edge. Suddenly there was a faint rustle in the rushes and a ripple of movement and a long, thin green creature whipped across their path. One end was pointed. The other end was flat with two eyes and a mouth and out of the mouth flickered a forked tongue.

"H-s-s-s! H-s-s-s!" hissed the long, thin, narrow green creature.

"Good morning," said Tammy and Lulu.

"H-s-s-s! H-s-s-s!" hissed the creature again. "Why don't you run away. I am a snake and snakes bite people."

"I'm not afraid of you," said Lulu. "You're only a green skipping-rope."

"And not a very good one," said Tammy, "because you haven't proper handles to hold."

"But I'm poisonous," said the snake. "Very, very poisonous. One bite, and you'll fall dead."

"I think you exaggerate," said Lulu. "I don't fall dead very easily."

"I can swallow an ox whole," went on the snake, wriggling with pride.

"Horns and all?" gasped Tammy.

"Horns and all."

"You must think we are very silly if we believe tales like that," said Tammy. "Swallow an ox indeed! You could hardly swallow an egg."

"Don't be cross because you haven't any handles," said Lulu kindly. "Some skipping-ropes haven't handles. You just wind the ends round your hands. Goodby."

"Goodby," said Tammy.

The children went on their way through the forest and the snake curled himself round the branch of a tree and looked puzzled.

"Well, I never did in all my born days!" he hissed to himself.

By this time Tammy and Lulu had explored enough

for one day and they turned around and went home the way they had come.

When they got back, they found their father was home and he and their mother were both looking for them and calling their names.

Their parents were too glad to see them safe and sound to be very cross.

"Where have you been?" asked their mother, hugging first Lulu and then Tammy.

"Yes, where have you been? Tell us!" said their father more sternly.

"We just went for a walk in the forest," said Tammy, "and we met an old gentleman in a fur coat with a bad cold. He said he was a bear and ate people, but of course we didn't believe *that*."

"Then we met someone else in a striped coat," said Lulu, "and he said he was a tiger, but he was only a big cat like Mitzi and we told him so. He pretended he ate people, too."

"Then we found a very big pincushion who wouldn't move out of our way," said Tammy, "and he boasted that everyone was scared of his prickles. He said he was a porcupine and could frighten a lion. But he didn't frighten us. We aren't frightened of pincushions even if they can talk."

"Then, last of all," said Lulu, "we came across a green skipping-rope who thought he was a snake, and a poisonous one, too. He told terrible stories and wanted us to believe that he could swallow an ox——"

"Horns and all," put in Tammy.

"Yes, horns and all. But we didn't believe a word he said."

"And we don't either," said their father and mother. "You are making it all up. If you had really met these fierce creatures you would never have got back alive."

"Well!" said the children when they were alone. "Well! We tell the truth and no one believes us, not even our own parents! Well! I never did in all my born days!"

The Snowman

"Pippa," said Miss Steel. "What have I just been saying?"

All the class turned and looked at Pippa, who blushed scarlet and hung her head.

"I—I'm afraid I don't know, Miss Steel."

"You don't know because you weren't paying attention to the lesson."

"No, Miss Steel. Yes, Miss Steel. I mean——"

"You mean you were thinking about something quite different. Something far more interesting than your seven times table. Tell us what it was."

"It was nothing, Miss Steel. Nothing at all."

"Then please stop thinking about nothing, and attend to the lesson instead."

"Yes, Miss Steel."

The class stopped looking at Pippa and turned to the blackboard again. Pippa's cheeks cooled as she, too, watched the white chalk writing rows of figures on the blackness. She had just told a lie, but she was not sorry. The truth would have been far worse. Everyone would have laughed at her and Miss Steel would have been even angrier if she had said that she was thinking about her snowman. Especially as he wasn't even made yet. But the moment school was over she was going to hurry home and begin him.

The bell rang at last, and the children sat still and straight and silent, so that Miss Steel would have no excuse for keeping them in to teach them a lesson on good manners.

"Good afternoon, children."

"Good afternoon, Miss Steel."

In a few seconds they were in the cloakroom, pushing their feet into boots, buttoning their coats like mad things, pulling on their gloves. Then out they ran into the playground which looked so different under its blanket of snow.

The playground had looked beautiful first thing in the morning, sparkling and smooth, with only a few footmarks leading from the gate to the door. Now, after two playtimes and a lunchhour, the snow was churned up and showed signs of great activity. There was a giant snowball which the big boys had made, rolling and rolling it till it was too heavy to roll another inch. It was as big as an armchair.

Then there were snowmen everywhere, most of them half-finished, or with their heads knocked off. Snowballs were piled by the wall, ammunition for a snow battle which had lasted till the bell rang, and which neither side had won.

As Pippa ran into the sharp, bright air, a girl stopped her.

"Are you staying to help roll a giant snowball? We're going to make one bigger than the boys made. Won't it be a surprise for them when they come to school tomorrow and see it?"

"No thanks, I have to go home," said Pippa.

Other friends asked her to go sliding on the pond, or sledding down the hill, but she shook her head.

"No thanks, not today. I have to hurry home."

She ran as fast as she could, slithering and staggering through the drifts. She lived in a cottage just outside the village, with a grassy patch in front, bounded by a low stone wall. This patch was where she intended to make her snowman, near to the wall, so that people passing by could see and admire him. There weren't many passers-by as the lane led only to a farm, but there would be the farm people and the postman and of course her father when he came home from work.

Pippa got the coal shovel and began work. The snow

was light and powdery, and she had to bang it down to make it stick. She worked hard, and when her mother called her to come in, she begged to stay out and not waste the daylight while it lasted.

"I can't possibly stop *now*. I want to get him finished before it gets too dark. Yes, I'd love sausages, later. No, I'm not cold or wet or tired."

When her father came up the path the snowman was nearly done. He was as tall as she was herself, and a good shape, broad on the ground, then thinner, and his shoulders sloping in just the right way. There was only his head to do.

"Shall I give you a hand, Pippa? This is a great snowman," said her father.

"Thanks Daddy, but I'd rather like to finish him by myself. When I've got his head on I'm coming in to eat with you. It's sausages tonight."

She heard her father stamping to get the snow off his boots while she made a roll of snow, patted it into a round ball for a head, and pressed it firmly on to the snowman's shoulders. To her dismay, it fell off. The second time she pressed harder, particularly along the part where his neck should have been. Her hands began to ache with cold, but she did not care. In a few minutes she would be indoors by the fire.

This time the head stayed in its place.

"I'll finish you tomorrow," said Pippa. "I'll try to get some clothes for you and everything. Perhaps I'll get up early and do it before I go to school."

She picked up the shovel and took it back to the coal bin. Then she turned and ran back to the snowman and put two pieces of coal where his eyes should be.

"Now you can have a good look around," she said, as she went indoors.

After supper, feeling warm and cozy, Pippa drew the curtains apart and looked out. It was a bright, frosty night. The snowman seemed taller than ever. She rubbed the misty marks of her breath off the glass and looked more carefully. Surely he'd grown. And he was so near, only a few steps from the window. But she'd made him away by the gate. She let the curtains fall together.

"Daddy, Mummy, do come and look! The snowman has moved. He's moved nearly up to the cottage."

Her father crossed the room and peered out.

"Seems all right to me. That's where he was when I came home, at any rate."

"Well, then, he's moved back in the minute since I first looked out."

"Time for bed." said her mother. "If you can see snowmen walking round the garden you must be overtired. Come along and have your bath."

She wouldn't agree to Pippa getting up early and finishing the snowman before breakfast.

"It's a long enough day as it is," she said firmly. "If you work hard at school, and play in the snow at playtime and then again when you get home, you'll have done enough."

When her mother had gone, Pippa got out of bed and went to the window. The snowman was just where she had made him. He stood, still and white and watchful. She slipped back into bed and while she was planning what she was going to do in the morning, she fell asleep.

Out in the garden the snowman stared at the cottage with his coal-black eyes.

The next day Miss Steel had her patience sorely tried. The girls came in after playtime with their hair soaking wet as the boys had pushed handfuls of snow down their necks. The ones with long hair had to be rubbed with towels and do their lessons with their hair spread out as if they were mermaids. The boys were scolded and strictly forbidden to put as much as a pinch of snow down anybody's neck.

So at lunch time the boys picked sides and built two snow forts where they could take shelter, and pelt the other side with snowballs. The girls helped by making ammunition and piling it up in reserve. The very little children had their playtime earlier and had decorated the window-sills with rows of snowpies, made with their seaside buckets.

Pippa joined in the snow battle, but all the time she was longing to get home. She had asked her mother at breakfast if there were any old clothes she could borrow, and her mother had told her that there was a bundle waiting to go to the rummage sale and she could look through it.

Pippa was sure she could find something suitable for her snowman.

When school was over, Pippa hurried home. The snowman looked even better than she had remembered. The bundle of rummage was on the kitchen table and she went through it. She was lucky as there was an old felt hat of her father's, and a ragged scarf knitted in stripes. She put the hat on the snowman's head and tied the scarf round his neck. Then she looked again. His face needed improving.

Two more bits of coal set close together made his nose, and the next thing was his mouth. She tried a row of bits of coal, but quickly removed them as it gave him a fierce expression. What would be better? She tried a twig, and some small stones, but these were not right either. Then, as a last attempt, she curved a slice of carrot.

"Thank you," said the snowman.

"I didn't know you could talk!" said Pippa.

"I couldn't till I had a mouth. I was afraid you might give up and leave me without one, and that wouldn't have done at all."

"Why wouldn't it have done?"

"Because I'm naturally a talkative fellow."

"Is there anything else I've forgotten?"

"No, I think I'm pretty well suited, thank you. Unless

it was something to wear in a buttonhole."

"But you haven't got a—"

"Don't say it! Don't say it!" interrupted the snowman. "I know I haven't a buttonhole to put a buttonhole in. But I never let a thing like that worry me."

Pippa looked anxiously round the wintry garden.

"A Christmas rose wouldn't show up much, being white, and a piece of laurel is rather dull. Would you like the sprig of holly that was stuck in the Christmas pudding? It's still in the kitchen."

"Yes, that would be very seasonable."

Pippa ran to the cottage and fetched the sprig. It was rather dried up and the red berries were beginning to wrinkle, but the snowman was delighted. Pippa stuck it in where his buttonhole would have been, if he'd had one, and he bent his head forward to admire the effect.

Pippa nearly cried out:

"Do be careful! Your head isn't any too safe!" but she just stopped herself in time. It might hurt his feelings.

"Now I'm the best snowman in the whole village," he went on proudly. "I have the most elegant figure. The most attractive face. The most stylish hat and the gayest muffler. And of course, the smartest buttonhole."

"You're certainly very nice," agreed Pippa, "but you mustn't be too sure that you're the best. That's boasting.

There might be, I don't say there is, but there might be one a teeny bit better; perhaps with a brand new hat and blue marbles for eyes and an umbrella that goes up and down."

"Well, there isn't, so there!" snapped the snowman.

"But I said there *might* be."

"And I say there isn't."

"You can't know. You're just guessing."

"I do know. What do you think I did last night while you were sleeping, tucked up in bed with your hot water bottle? Do you think I stood here like a statue, bored stiff and no one to talk to? Not a bit of it! I explored the whole village and visited every snowman in the place. Every single one."

"So you can move about," said Pippa. "And did you move up to the sitting-room window after supper?"

"Of course I did. I wanted to see what you were all up to. But I didn't stay long. The sight of that roaring fire made me feel quite faint. I almost thought I might melt, even from looking at it, and I ran quickly back to my place by the gate. I soon calmed down. The north wind was blowing and there was a pleasant nip in the air. Just what I enjoy."

"I'm glad I made you some eyes before I went in."

"So am I! So am I! I was hoping I could have a look

round and go for a prowl. You're a good, thoughtful girl. I can assure you that there isn't another snowman in the village to compare with me. They're a sorry lot."

"What's wrong with them?" asked Pippa.

"Some are so small that people keep tripping over them. Some have no heads. Some haven't eyes—or mouths—or clothes. But there are good fellows among them. I look forward to tonight when I shall visit them again. There were some very sad cases, though."

"Why were they sad cases?"

"One was made in the middle of the pavement and the lady of the house told her son to knock him down with the poker as someone might run into him in the dark. Another was pelted with snowballs till his head rolled off."

The snowman looked so upset that Pippa tried to think of a way of cheering him up.

"Would you care to smoke a pipe? You could smoke my clay bubble pipe if you like."

The snowman smiled.

"Yes, that would be a great treat. Run indoors and get it, there's a good girl. And don't forget the tobacco!" he added, as Pippa went off.

Pippa found the pipe at once but she did not know what to do about the tobacco. Then she had an idea. She took her father's pouch from the shelf where it lay beside

his pipe, and stuffed a pinch of the tobacco into the bowl of the clay pipe.

The snowman was delighted.

"Real tobacco!" he sighed, breathing in deeply. "Best quality, I'll be bound. I shall allow all my friends to have a sniff when I visit them tonight. Snowmen don't often have real tobacco. They have to make do with sand or sawdust or something like that."

His smile stretched right across his face, and his black eyes shone with pride.

The weather stayed cold and there was no sign of the snow melting. Pippa ran home from school each day, anxious to see her snowman and have a chat with him. He was very fond of stories and she told him all she could remember. He particularly liked *The Snow Queen* and any story that mentioned snow or ice or winter. He learned to sing:

> The north wind doth blow
> And we shall have snow,
> And what will the robin do then, poor thing.
> He'll sit in a barn
> To keep himself warm,
> And hide his head under his wing, poor thing.

The snowman really did think the robin was a "poor thing" to make such a fuss about the north wind, which was his favorite wind.

Pippa took to playing in the snowman's part of the garden, making snow dens and snow walls, so that her parents would not suspect what was really going on. Once, she suggested to the snowman that her father and mother would like to meet him, but he became very huffy and turned his head away and refused to speak. It took her quite ten minutes to bring him around again. When he did open his mouth his voice was sharp with anger.

"Isn't it enough," he stormed, "that I talk to you? Isn't it enough? Most people live all their lives without even once hearing a snowman speak, and you hear me every day. And now you want to show me off to every Tom, Dick and Harry in the village."

"I don't! I don't!" shouted Pippa, nearly as angry herself. "I only wanted to introduce you, very politely, to my parents."

"Well, you can't, and that's flat. No self-respecting snowman ever speaks to a grown person. Why, I know a snowman who once said 'good morning' to a lady, and she went straight off to her doctor and complained that she was ill and hearing voices."

Pippa promised that she would never try to introduce him to anyone, ever, and he gradually calmed down. She made a snow bench nearby, where he could sit if he wanted to. He was pleased with this, and told her later that he often used it during the night, sometimes sharing it with a friend.

"I am the only snowman in the village who can offer such hospitality," he said proudly. "I can offer a seat to sit on, a sniff of real tobacco, and I can tell stories and sing songs."

"Do you like being called 'Snowman'?" said Pippa one day.

"I don't mind. It's what I am."

"But it's rather as if you called me 'girl' and I'd much rather be called 'Pippa'. Wouldn't you like a name of your own?"

"Why not?" said the snowman. "What do you suggest?"

"Frosty, perhaps?"

"Sounds like a dog. I want a proper name."

"George, or William, or Charles? They are all names of kings."

"I don't fancy them."

"What about Peterkin?"

"That will do. I feel like Peterkin. I believe I look like Peterkin. Do I look like Peterkin?"

"The very image," said Pippa.

"Please write it for me in the snow."

So Pippa found a stick and wrote PETERKIN across the lawn, in large letters. The snowman was delighted and insisted on being taught to spell it himself. He was quick to learn and could soon rattle off: P-E-T-E-R-K-I-N and point to any of the letters if asked.

"If I stayed here long enough you could teach me to read," he said. "How long did it take you to learn?"

"About a year, I think," said Pippa. "That is, before I could read to myself."

"I shan't be here as long as that, so it isn't worth beginning," said Peterkin. "Snowmen often stay only for a day or two. I've been very fortunate to be here so long. Very fortunate indeed. And I'm as hard and firm as the day you made me."

He patted his chest with a flat white hand.

"Would you like to come with me tonight to the Snowmen's Jamboree?"

"Yes, I would," said Pippa, "but I don't know what a jamboree is."

"Oh, it's just a meeting. We meet in the middle of the

woods where we're not likely to be disturbed. We have to start from here at midnight."

"It's rather late for me," said Pippa.

"Can't be helped," said Peterkin. "If we left any earlier we might be missed. Some of us live very near doors and windows and when people put out the cat, or the milk bottles, or give the dog a run, they would be alarmed if we were not in our usual places. They might come and look for us. It would lead to all kinds of trouble. Why, we should never hear the end of it. The police might be called in."

"I'll try to stay awake," said Pippa doubtfully. "I can listen to the church clock striking."

"Don't do that," said Peterkin. "Get to sleep as soon as you can and then you'll be fresh as a snowflake when I wake you. I'll throw a snowball at your window."

"Thank you," said Pippa. "I'll go to bed with some of my clothes on and then it will only take a jiffy to slip into the top ones."

They played in the snow till Pippa's mother called her in to tea. Pippa intended to lie awake, in case she did not hear the snowball hit the window, but her bed was so warm and comfortable that she fell asleep at once.

She thought she had been asleep only a few minutes when she heard a dull thud and her window rattled. For a second she was frightened. Then she remembered. Peterkin. The snowball. The Snowmen's Jamboree.

She tugged on her thick trousers and two jerseys, and tiptoed downstairs into the hall for her duffle coat and boots. Then she opened the front door as quietly as she could. Peterkin stood outside.

"How cold," whispered Pippa, as the icy wind touched her face and seemed to blow right through her clothes. "How cold!" Her teeth began to chatter.

"I find it just pleasant," said Peterkin, "but I know it's different for you. Would you mind if I gave you a hug? You would find it a great help."

"All right. If you want to," said Pippa, not very willingly.

Peterkin wrapped his long white arms round her and she was tightly pressed to his cold body, her cheek against his icy cheek. For a second the cold was so intense that she wanted to scream. Then, as he let her go, a wonderful change came over her, spreading from her face downwards, out to her fingers and toes.

"I don't feel cold any more," she gasped in surprise. "I don't feel anything! It's like magic!"

"We must get moving," said Peterkin. "Come along."

He took her hand in his and glided away down the path, along the lane, following the footpath leading to the woods. His snowy fingers did not feel cold, grasping her warm ones. Just firm and hard. Other gliding white shapes joined them and they moved in single file through the wood. When they reached the clearing by the plank bridge over the stream, they stopped.

The woodcutters had been at work and there were piles of logs and single tree trunks lying on the ground, white with snow. These the snowmen used as seats. They were, as Peterkin had said, a very mixed lot. A few were well shaped with proper faces, but a great many had eyes, or nose, or mouth, or even all three, missing. Some had no head and were just like white posts. The ones without mouths nodded or shook their heads and managed, very cleverly, to make themselves understood.

Peterkin introduced Pippa who shook hands with them

all and exchanged a few remarks about the weather. They begged her to sing them a song as Peterkin had boasted about her singing. It was hard to think of something suitable at a moment's notice and she could only remember a song about a fox.

A fox went out on a chilly night
And prayed for the moon to give him light,
For he'd many a mile to go that night
Before he reached the Town-O!
The Town-O! the Town-O!
He'd many a mile to go that night
Before he reached the Town-O!

The snowmen joined in the chorus and clapped their hands at the end. Their snowy palms made a queer, dull sound but there was no doubt that they were pleased.

"Won't you sing to me now?" said Pippa. "It's your turn."

"We will sing the Snowmen's Song," said Peterkin.

The snowmen arranged themselves like a choir, the shorter ones in front and the taller ones at the back. Peterkin broke a straight twig from a tree, shook the snow off it, and began to conduct. The unlucky snowmen without mouths nodded their heads in time to the song, and the ones without heads swayed from side to side.

We are the snowmen, cold and white,
We sleep by day and we play by night,
Sliding and gliding round and round
We leave no trace on the frozen ground.

Little and big ones, thin and fat,
Some with a scarf and some with a hat,
Some with eyes and nose in place,
Others with nothing but a plain white face.

We have our fun while children sleep,
Up to the window panes we creep,
Peer at the lighted room inside,
Then back to our place in the snow we glide.

Now it was Pippa's turn to clap, which she did with all her might, surprised that her hands had no feeling as she struck them together.

The serious part of the jamboree was over, and the snowmen began to enjoy themselves in their own way. Some slid in a line on the frozen stream, each holding on to the shoulder of the one in front. Others climbed on the piles of logs and jumped off into a deep snow drift which was soft as a feather bed. Pippa played hide-and-seek with a group, but it was difficult for her to find them in their white clothes, and they found her far too easily in her red duffle coat and hood.

When the church clock struck five the games stopped. The snowmen brushed bits of leaf and twig off themselves, patted their hair into place, and got into single file for the homeward journey. Peterkin led and Pippa came next, running to keep up with his fast, smooth glide. When they reached the lane, each snowman said goodnight to Peterkin and Pippa, and had a sniff of Peterkin's pipe of real tobacco as a farewell treat.

"Is there another jamboree tomorrow?" asked Pippa, as they opened the garden gate.

"Yes, and it might be the last. This cold snap can't go on for ever. Would you like to come?"

"Yes, I would," said Pippa, who had a private reason for wanting to be there. A wonderful plan was forming in her mind, but she was suddenly too sleepy to think it out just then. In the morning her mind would be clearer.

The next day, on the way to school, Pippa recognised several of the snowmen she had met the night before. She was walking with some friends and none of the snowmen spoke, but each gave a sign of greeting. One nodded. One smiled. One winked. And a very daring one waved.

When school was over in the afternoon and Pippa had run home as usual, she found Peterkin rather quiet.

"Is anything wrong, Peterkin?"

"No, I don't think so."

"Has anyone been horrid to you, thrown a stone at you, or anything like that?"

"No, no one has been horrid."

"Or perhaps—perhaps someone said something you didn't like? Don't fret. I'm sure they didn't mean it."

"No, it isn't that. In fact people have said nice things, all the nicer because they had no idea that I understood what they were saying. The postman said I was a fine figure of a snowman. The newspaper boy sniffed my pipe and said: 'Gosh! Real tobacco!' And a baby in a buggy called out, 'Daddy snowman!' "

"Tell me what's wrong, Peterkin. We're friends, aren't we? And friends tell each other everything."

"Then look at the icicles on the gate."

Pippa looked. She often broke one off and sucked it, so she knew just what they were like.

"They're a bit shorter."

"Yes, they are. When the sun was out earlier in the day the tips began to melt and drops of water formed. We have a proverb which says: *When icicles drip, away snowmen slip.*"

"But not yet, Peterkin. Not yet. You're as good as new." And she patted him on the shoulder to prove it.

"Nearly as good as new. The sun gave me a slight headache this morning."

"But you'll come to the jamboree tonight, won't you?"

Peterkin gave himself a shake as if to get rid of unpleasant thoughts.

"Of course I shall come, and you with me. We shall all be there, never fear. I hope you'll sing your fox song again; it has been running through my head all day long but there are one or two words I've forgotten."

"And you must all sing your snowmen song. I've been trying to remember that too. Will you wake me at midnight as you did before?"

"Yes. On the very stroke."

They played a game of noughts and crosses which Peterkin won and that put him in a good mood. Pippa felt reassured when she had to go indoors. He seemed his old, cheerful self.

Before she went to bed, Pippa took an old shoulder bag and went round the house collecting small objects from different places. Sometimes she stopped to think, and to count and recount them. When she was satisfied she hung the bag on a peg in the hall, underneath her duffle coat. It was completely hidden from anyone passing by.

As before, she felt she had only been asleep for a few minutes when there was the dull thud and the window rattled. She dressed quickly and crept downstairs, slung the bag over her shoulder, and went out into the garden. It was cold, but not the piercing cold of the previous night.

"You'd better let me give you a hug," said Peterkin, holding out his white arms. "It will be cold in the clearing."

Once again he pressed her tightly to him and she felt the terrible icy shiver going through her. Then all was well. She felt nothing at all as they set off together, hand in hand, Peterkin gliding swiftly and she hurrying to keep up. Other snowmen joined them and when they reached the clearing it was full of white shapes.

The other snowmen greeted her like an old friend. Although they chatted and told jokes, she felt they were not quite as carefree as they had been the night before. She saw one pointing out to another a row of icicles on the bridge. He was saying: "Have you noticed that they've shrunk?"

And the second one answered regretfully: "*When icicles drip, away snowmen slip.*"

When they asked Pippa to sing her song about the fox, she unslung her bag, and said:

"Before I sing, I've brought a few little presents for you.

Not very much, but things you may find useful. Will you stand in a circle and then I'll give them out."

The snowmen looked pleased and when they had made their circle they could hardly keep still for excitement.

Pippa began with a small snowman who had no face at all, just a blank.

"I expect you'd like to see—" she gave him two coal eyes.

"And smell——" she gave him a nose.

"And talk——" she gave him a curved, orange-peel mouth.

"Thank you, thank you," he said happily, turning his head to look around. "Why, you're even prettier than I had imagined now I can see you. And I shall be able to smell Peterkin's tobacco with my new nose. And I can sing the Snowm n's Song with the others. I'm the happiest snowman in the village," and he began turning round and round with joy, like a top.

The next one needed a mouth too. The next one had only one eye and needed a second. Everyone in the circle was given something. The ones who had proper faces were pleased with a real button for their waistcoat, or a wisp of wool for a moustache. Peterkin carried the bag for her on his snowy shoulder, and would not accept anything for himself, not even an extra button. "I have all a snowman could possibly want," he whispered.

The snowmen took their seats on the logs while Pippa sang her song.

A fox went out on a chilly night
And prayed for the moon to give him light,
For he'd many a mile to go that night
Before he reached the Town-O!
The Town-O! the Town-O!
He'd many a mile to go that night
Before he reached the Town-O!

This time everyone could join in the chorus. Then they stood up in their choir formation and sang their own snowmen song. Pippa found she remembered almost all of it and could join in, while Peterkin conducted.

We are the snowmen, cold and white,
We sleep by day and we play by night,
Sliding and gliding round and round
We leave no trace on the frozen ground.

Little and big ones, thin and fat,
Some with a scarf and some with a hat,
Some with eyes and nose in place,
Others with nothing but a plain white face.

We have our fun while children sleep,
Up to the window panes we creep,
Peer at the lighted rooms inside,
Then back to our place in the snow we glide.

"It isn't true now," said the very small snowman. "We *all* have faces!"

Afterwards they slid and hid and chased each other, and tumbled in the drifts, and the wood rang with their shouts. But when the village clock struck five, they started for home, gliding through the wood in single file.

Pippa and Peterkin said goodnight outside Pippa's door.

"It was the best night of my life," said Peterkin.

"And the best of mine," said Pippa.

As they stood together they heard a faint drip—drip—drip. The thaw was beginning.

The next day the icicles on the gate almost disappeared. The snow was softer and the children's feet sank in. The village street was slushy with churned-up snow.

When Pippa came home after school she looked very carefully at the snowmen she passed. They were almost the same, but she noticed small changes. Faces were slightly lop-sided. The slope of shoulders was different. Eyes were no longer on an exact level, and a button or two had dropped off waistcoats.

She rushed up to Peterkin and looked at him without speaking. His round face had altered its shape and his hat seemed too big for him. But his expression was just the same, kind and cheerful. Her eyes filled with tears and she turned her head away. At once he laid his hand on her arm and said gently:

"Come, come, Pippa, there's no need to be sad. I'm not grieving, so why should you?"

"I don't want you to—to go away!" said Pippa. "I want you to stay for ever."

"But you know I can't do that. I felt sick today when the sun shone, even protected by my hat. I should be very ill indeed if I stayed much longer. Snowmen can only live in the snow."

"I can't bear you just to disappear, just to melt and melt till there's nothing left."

"When I melt, I start another life, didn't you know? I shall float up into the sky and turn into a cloud. All snowmen turn into clouds. I've enjoyed being down here, and knowing you, and having fun, but I shall enjoy sailing across the sky, too. I shall take strange shapes as I float along. Sometimes I shall be a ship with white sails. Sometimes a swan or a dragon. You can look up and watch me."

"I don't mind so much now I understand," said Pippa, "but I still mind your going. I shall miss you."

"And I shall miss you too. But I haven't gone yet. We may have several days together still. Don't worry if I look peculiar and unlike myself. It takes a long time to turn into a cloud. And don't, whatever you do, be sad. I can't bear that!"

Peterkin sniffed and blinked and rubbed his eyes, and looked very miserable himself.

For nearly a week Peterkin and the other snowmen stood and shrank and changed. The small ones disappeared first. Heads rolled off and bodies dwindled till there was only a hump left. Then that, too, vanished.

Pippa learned another snowman proverb when she heard Peterkin say to a friend, as melting snow water gushed down the lane: "*When waters flow, snowmen must go.*"

Peterkin lasted longer than any other snowman in the village. He had been well made, and the wall gave him some shade and shelter. But gradually he grew shorter, and thinner, and lost his fine figure, till he was only a white post, then a hump of snow, and then nothing at all.

The day that Peterkin finally left the garden was bright and sunny and would certainly have given him a headache. Pippa felt strange going along the path and out of the gate without his friendly and familiar smile, or a wave of his hand.

When playtime came, and the children ran out into the sunshine, there were rolling white clouds in the blue sky. Most of the girls had brought skipping-ropes, and the boys were making paper darts, but Pippa stood alone, looking upwards. Which cloud was Peterkin, she wondered? There were so many to choose from. There were feather cushions and feather beds. There was something with long horns, and a bird, and a tower. Then she saw him, a tall figure with outstretched arms, hurrying forward, ahead of the others.

"Just like Peterkin. He always wanted to be first," she thought, and smiled.

Aunt Nag

Once upon a time, a princess and a prince were playing in the palace garden. Tika, the princess, saw a scarlet butterfly with silver dots on its wings, fluttering from

flower to flower.

"Look, Paul!" she cried to her little brother. "Look at the pretty butterfly!"

The children ran to get a closer view, but as they drew near the rose where the butterfly was resting, it flew on to a spray of honeysuckle, then to a sprig of lilac, then over the hedge which made a thick green wall round the garden.

"I know where we can get through," said Paul, lying

full length on the grass and disappearing through a gap at the foot of the hedge. Tika followed him and they saw the butterfly settling on a sunny stone. But in a second it was off once more, the children following, fluttering through the patches of light and shadow made by the sun falling through the branches. In the sun the silver spots shone like stars. In the shadow they were almost invisible.

The butterfly was tireless and never came to rest for more than an instant. Sometimes it fanned its wings as if to cool itself, or hovered just above a flower head as if making up its mind, but always it fluttered on, further into the forest. Tika and Paul, following it, were soon breathless and weary.

When the butterfly crossed a stream and settled on a water-lily leaf, the children lay down on the soft grass of the bank to get cool. The bees hummed on the water mint, a bird chirped drowsily among the willows, and they felt drowsy too. Soon they were asleep.

When they opened their eyes the butterfly had gone, the sun had set and the water in the stream was dark. No bee buzzed and no bird sang. They were lost, and even when the moon rose they had no idea which way to go. They had never before been outside the palace grounds except when driving in the royal carriage with their parents.

There were rustlings in the bushes and an occasional growl from the shadows, and Tika and Paul began to imagine wild beasts waiting to pounce on them. So they climbed one of the willow trees for safety and clung there all night, shivering and weeping.

The next morning they drank from the stream and ate a few wild raspberries and tried to find their way home. But they only went deeper and deeper into the forest. They pushed their way through thickets and climbed over fallen trees. They picked their way across swamps where the warning cotton grass grew, and plodded up to their knees through soft carpets of dead leaves. Again they spent the night in a tree, too cold and frightened to sleep.

The following day they were almost too tired to drag their weary feet, but they pressed on slowly, Tika encouraging little Paul.

"We will take fifty more steps," she said, and when the fifty were taken they attempted forty more, then thirty, then twenty, then ten. When Paul still lagged behind and whimpered that his feet hurt, Tika knew they must soon give up hope of getting home and sit down and wait for whatever came.

Just then they came upon a clearing, and in the clearing was a cottage. The garden was full of thistles and there were cobwebs over the windows, but it had a gate, even if a broken one, and a door, though there was no knocker. Best of all, smoke was curling from the crooked chimney.

"Someone is living there—someone will help us!" said Tika, pulling Paul by the hand. She knocked on the door with her knuckles, but the sound was so soft that no one came. Then she picked up a stone and knocked loudly.

A cracked voice from within replied:

"Who knocks with bone
And then with stone?"

"It is I, Tika, and my brother Paul," said Tika. "We are lost and tired. Please let us in."

The door opened and the children saw a bent old woman with a big hooked nose and a black cat rubbing round her thin legs. The cat arched his back and spat when he saw the children.

"Come in! Come in! My little ones, my angels!" said the old woman. "Come in, Tika and Paul. I am your Aunt Nag."

"I didn't know we had an Aunt Nag," said Tika, but she was much too tired to argue and she and Paul drank the hot, bitter drink Aunt Nag made for them, and ate the hard, burned bread, and fell asleep in the goose-feather bed which seemed the most comfortable thing in the house.

For three days Aunt Nag took care of them, bringing them meals and telling them to rest and not to worry about anything, but on the fourth day she changed her tone.

"You are quite well now," she said sharply. "Get up and set to work. You, Tika, clean the windows (but don't break the cobwebs as it's unlucky to spoil a cobweb). You, Paul, go into the garden and tidy it up (but don't cut down the thistles as they are my favorite flowers)."

The children did their best, but the windows were covered with grime and it was impossible not to break a cobweb or two while cleaning them. As for the garden, it was like a jungle, and Paul's hands and legs were soon scratched and bleeding from the prickly thistles. Aunt Nag grumbled at them all the time. They were slow, clumsy, stupid, idle, ungrateful, and many other unpleasant things. The cat made things worse by scratching Tika as she rubbed the windows, and biting Paul as he weeded.

When the long day was over and the children were having their supper, Tika said to Aunt Nag:

"May Paul and I go home tomorrow? Our father and mother will be missing us and looking everywhere."

"You came here by yourselves and you'll have to get home by yourselves," said Aunt Nag, "and I expect your parents are used to being without you by now. Children are a great trouble to bring up."

"My father and mother will never be used to being without me," said Paul, "and I don't believe you're my aunt at all. You don't look like an aunt or behave like an aunt. Why have we never seen you before?"

"People who ask too many questions never get any answers," replied Aunt Nag. "Now go to bed, because I want you to work hard tomorrow."

"She isn't our aunt," whispered Paul to Tika, under the blankets. "I think she's a witch."

"So do I," said Tika, "and that's why the cat spits and scratches and won't be friends. We'll run away when we get a chance."

Aunt Nag kept an eagle in a cage. The cat brought it home when it was a little eaglet and could not fly. Only a witch's cat could have climbed the steep crag and carried his prey such a long way home. Now, though the eagle had never stretched his wings in flight, he perched as high as he could in his cage, staring at the sky with sad, golden eyes.

The next day, while Aunt Nag was busy gathering herbs to make a brew, the eagle said to the children:

"Let me out. Open the cage door. I want to fly. I will find the palace where you live and bring you news of your father and mother." Tika opened the door of the cage and the eagle flapped clumsily out. He spread his wings once or twice, like a person stretching, and then, fixing his golden eyes on the sun, he soared away.

"We will wait till the eagle comes back," said Tika, scraping at a big cauldron that Aunt Nag had ordered her to scour.

"Yes, I hope he is quick," sighed Paul, returning to his thistles.

Aunt Nag was angry to find the eagle had escaped, but the children were working so hard she never suspected they had opened the cage door. Also, she now took a delight in saying to Tika or Paul, "If you don't behave I shall shut you in the eagle's cage."

Two days later the eagle returned, but he dared not loiter as Aunt Nag was in the house and the cat sitting by the gate. He fell out of the sky like a stone, hurtling towards the earth, and landed at Paul's feet.

"Your father and his men are searching far and wide," he whispered, "and your mother weeps day and night."

"Which way do we go to get home?" asked Paul as Aunt Nag came out to pick some nettles.

"To the sunset! To the sunset!" said the eagle, spreading his wings and soaring into the blue. Aunt Nag saw his great shadow as he rose and she ran out, but was too late to clutch even a feather.

"Why didn't you hold him, you stupid child!" she said to Paul, cuffing him with her yellow hand.

"To the sunset" was not much to go on, but it was enough for the children. They got up in the middle of the night and crept out of the house, not daring to take even a crust of bread as the doors and cupboards creaked so loudly. They had oiled the hinges of the gate the day before because these squeaked the loudest of all. The two children could not travel very fast in the darkness but they set out toward the west where the sun had set.

At last the morning came and the sun rose behind them and shone on their backs, warming and cheering them. Soon they began to feel hungry. Even Aunt Nag's burned bread would have seemed a feast. They picked a leaf here and there and chewed it, but some of the leaves were hot and bitter and Tika feared they might be poisonous. Then they came to a cherry tree, the fruit shining like jewels.

"Please, cherry tree, may we have some of your cherries?" asked the children, bowing low.

"Yes, all you can eat," replied the cherry tree, bending down its branches. The children gathered what they wanted and ate thankfully. Then, to repay the tree for its kindness, they planted the stones in the soft soil.

"One day you will be queen of a cherry orchard," they said, and the tree was glad as it had no other cherry tree to talk to and was lonely.

Aunt Nag had wakened by now and found the children gone, and she and her cat set out to catch them and bring them back. The cat ran on ahead to track the children's footprints and Aunt Nag followed. When they reached the cherry tree Aunt Nag was tempted by the ripe fruit.

She seized the tree and shook it roughly, tearing off any boughs she could reach, fruit, leaves, stalks and all, while the cat sharpened his claws on the trunk.

Then the tree sent down a shower of cherry stones like bullets, hitting Aunt Nag fiercely on the face and making the cat spit and swear, so the two hurried on without having tasted a single cherry.

The children felt better for their meal of cherries and they went on quickly, but the sun became so hot and the air in the forest so heavy, that they longed for a drink. There was no sign of a stream and even the flowers they passed had no dewdrop in their cups. Their mouths were dry and Tika gave Paul a pebble to suck and sucked one herself, but it was water they needed, fresh, cool water.

Suddenly Paul's foot struck something hard and he found it was part of a circle of stones built into a low wall. He peered over the wall and saw, far below, the gleam of water. Tika dropped her pebble over the edge and Paul did the same. They waited and heard the echo of two splashes.

"It is a well!" they cried together. "A well of water!" But how were they to reach the water with no rope and no bucket?

"Dear well," pleaded Tika, "we are very thirsty. Can you spare some of your water?" and she and Paul bowed low. There was a rushing, gushing sound and a jet of water shot up as high as the wall, like a fountain. They leaned over and drank in turn, Paul first and then Tika. When they had had all they needed, the jet sank down.

Tika twisted a wreath of blue flowers and threw it into the water and the well was glad because it was the first present it had ever been given.

Soon afterwards Aunt Nag and her cat came to the well and they, too, were thirsty. When they saw how far out of reach the water was, the cat spat and swore and Aunt Nag threw in lumps of earth, she was so angry, and declared that if *she* couldn't drink, then no one else should either. There was a rushing, gushing sound and a great wave rose and overflowed the wall and drenched Aunt Nag and her cat. They went on their way shaking themselves and grumbling.

The children managed to keep ahead till twilight fell and they could not see where to go. The cat could see in the dark so he and his mistress drew nearer and nearer. The children could see the cat's eyes glowing like two green lamps and they heard Aunt Nag gasping for breath as she hurried to keep up with him.

They found themselves at the foot of a high, rocky cliff, towering above them, so steep and rough that even in daylight it would have been difficult to climb. In the dark it was impossible.

"Hide us, great rock!" begged Tika, and she and Paul bowed low. "We are alone and weak and you are strong. Hide us, oh rock!"

Then a wide crack opened like a door and the children crept inside and the rock closed behind them. They were in a cave with moss on the floor and walls and roof of rock. A little waterfall fell like a white ribbon at one end, fringed with ferns. They lay down side by side on moss as soft as the goose-feather bed, and slept till morning.

When the cat found that the trail stopped at the rock, he

and Aunt Nag settled for the night under a bush, planning what they would do to the children when they caught them.

When the sun rose, the crack in the rock widened so that Tika and Paul could get through. Then it closed behind them.

"How can we thank you for taking care of us?" asked Tika.

"I have all I want," said the rock. "I have moss and ferns and a waterfall. What else could I want?"

"Would you like a name of your own?" said Tika.

"Yes, indeed," said the rock. "I did not know such a thing was possible. But I can't think of one. Will you choose one for me?"

"We'll call you the Rock of the Silver Buckle," said Tika, pulling the buckle off her belt. "I'll bury my buckle here in the moss," and she buried it as deeply as she could. As the children went on they heard the little waterfall singing: "Silver buckle, silver buckle, silver buckle," as it fell down the rock.

When Aunt Nag and the cat woke up, the cat was able to follow the trail to the very spot where the rock had opened. They could see a faint crack like the hinge of a door. "Let us in!" screamed Aunt Nag, and she hit the place with a stone and chipped a rough flake off the rock's smooth face. The cat scratched up any rock plants he could find, pinks and pennywort and stone-crop.

"Very well, come in!" rumbled the rock, opening a crack, "and never go out again," he added, closing it with Aunt Nag and the cat imprisoned inside. But as he did not like witches or witches' cats, he changed them into a mouse

and a beetle. There they live to this day, hiding from the sunshine, afraid that the eagle with his golden eyes and strong beak may see them and snap them up.

Safe from their pursuers, Tika and Paul went on their way in peace, guided by the eagle who flew overhead like a speck in the blue, swooping down to help them if they took a wrong turning. The next morning they saw the walls and towers of the palace and they ran through the iron gates and up the drive into the queen's arms.

Their father and mother assured them they had never had an aunt named Nag and that, beyond doubt, she was a witch.

As they walked together round the garden they saw the scarlet butterfly with silver spots on its wings, resting on a leaf.

"We've everything we want at home," said Tika, "even the butterfly that led us so far."

When the children were bigger and stronger, they explored the forest with their father's men. They found the cherry tree with an orchard of young trees around her, like a queen surrounded by her maidens. They found the well, too, and the men fixed a bucket and a chain so any traveler might drink. They even found the Rock of the Silver Buckle. The eagle had made his eyrie at the top and lived there with his mate.

But they never found the cottage with the broken gate and cobwebbed windows and prickly garden.

The Mud Boy

There was once a little black boy who lived in a village in the forest. He spent most of the day playing outside, but at night he slept in a round mud hut with the rest of the family. There were his grandfather and grandmother, his father and mother, and seven big brothers and sisters, all sleeping in the hut together. He was the youngest in the family and his name was Logo.

Because Logo was the youngest and smallest, the bigger ones did not think he needed much room. At night he had hardly enough space on the floor to stretch out comfortably, and he had to roll himself up into a ball.

When Logo's mother served the soup out of the big black pot which stood on the fire, they all held out their bowls made of half coconuts and she filled each bowl in turn, beginning with the old grandfather. Logo had his turn last of all and his bowl was the smallest of all. It was made from half of a very small coconut.

"When you are bigger you can have a bigger bowl," said his mother.

"When you are bigger you can come hunting with me," said his father.

"When you are bigger you can come with us and herd the cattle," said his brothers.

"When you are bigger you can come down to the river with us when we fill our calabashes," said his sisters.

But Logo was very small and everyone else was very big. His grandfather measured him against a tree and made a notch on the trunk level with the top of his head. Logo made his grandfather measure him every day and sometimes twice a day, but he did not seem to get any taller, and his grandfather grew angry at being disturbed so often from a comfortable doze to come out into the hot sun.

"I won't measure you till the next full moon," he said crossly.

Logo amused himself as best he could, but he was often very lonely. His brothers and sisters had real, hard, important work to do and they walked proudly about the village, cutting switches for driving the cattle, or carrying water on their heads in calabashes. He could only play with pebbles or gather sweet-scented flowers for his grandmother to smell. She was blind and this was her only way of enjoying the flowers that grew in the forest, the lilies as large as silver trumpets and the water mints strong as peppermint.

One day, Logo decided to make another little boy to be a companion. He made this other boy of bundles of tall grass, tied tightly round with creeper to make a round knob for a head, and a bundle for a body, and thinner bundles for arms and legs. He knew of a plant with sticky seeds and he stuck some of these on the face to make two eyes, a nose, and a row of teeth.

All day long he played with his new grassy companion and he was not lonely any more. But when he brought the Grass Boy into the hut at bedtime, there were cries of:

"Something is tickling my feet!"

"Something is tickling my neck!"

"Something is tickling my back!"

"Ugh! Ugh! It's Logo's bundle of grass! Put it outside, Logo, and you can play with it when you wake up."

So Logo sadly carried the Grass Boy outside and laid him near the fire which was kept burning night and day.

Logo woke early and ran out to fetch his companion. But what had happened? Where was Grass Boy? A cow had pushed her way out of the compound where the cows slept at night, and she was standing by the fire, contentedly munching something. Long bits of grass were hanging out of her mouth like long green whiskers. She put out her tongue and gathered the grassy fringe inside.

Logo cried so much that he could hardly eat his breakfast, but everyone said:

"Fancy crying for a bundle of grass! What a baby you are!"

Then Logo decided to make another little boy to be a companion. This time he made him of ferns. He chose ferns with broad, thick leaves and rolled them up tightly to make the various parts, the head and body, the arms and legs. He fastened the rolls with long, sharp thorns, like pins, to keep them together. He put little feathery ferns round the head to look like hair. He used white seeds for the face, for the eyes and nose and mouth. This Fern Boy was even better than the Grass Boy and Logo played with him all day long. He did not feel lonely any more.

At night, in the hut, as Logo lay with Fern Boy beside him, there were cries of:

"Something is scratching my feet!"

"Something is scratching my neck!"

"Something is scratching my back!"

"Ugh! Ugh! It's Logo's bundle of ferns. Put it outside, Logo, and you can play with it when you wake up!"

But Logo did not want to put Fern Boy outside. He just wriggled his way towards the door of the hut and

lay with Fern Boy in his arms, in the doorway, held so no one could complain of being scratched.

Logo woke up when the sun shone on his face. He sat up and rubbed his eyes. Something was wrong. Where was his new friend? He was nowhere to be seen. Then Logo heard busy chattering in the tree-tops and he looked up and there were the monkey people, squabbling and jabbering together, quarreling over Fern Boy. They snatched him from one to the other with their skinny hands and soon he was in shreds and tatters. Logo cried so much that he could not eat any breakfast at all and everyone said: "Fancy crying for a bundle of ferns! What a baby you are!"

Logo felt so lonely that he decided to make a little boy of sticks. This was more difficult, but it was a better idea than grass or ferns. The head was a black fir cone. The body was a thick stick and the arms and legs were thin ones. He made holes through the ends of the arms and legs and threaded wiry bits of creeper through the holes. Then he made more holes in the body and tied the arms and legs on with tight knots. He bit off the loose ends with his sharp white teeth. Then his new friend was finished.

The Stick Boy seemed as if he were alive. When Logo jigged him up and down, his arms jerked and his legs jerked and he looked as if he were dancing. Logo played with him all day long and he did not feel lonely any more. At night he hung him safely on a wooden peg that his father had driven into the wall of the hut. He was in nobody's way, hung up high, and not even the mischievous monkeys dared to come right inside the hut when it was full of people. The cows could not get in either as the door was too low for them to squeeze through.

Logo played with Stick Boy for a week. He talked to him and sang to him and Stick Boy was always ready to dance. He was never tired or cross or sleepy like other people.

One day Logo left Stick Boy by the fire while he went to pick some sweet-scented flowers for his blind grand-

mother. When he got back, his mother was poking the fire and peering into the pot of soup and grumbling:

"How do you expect me to cook soup for your supper if I have no sticks for the fire?"

It was Logo's job to collect sticks, so it was not surprising that she was displeased. "You left me only a handful of wretched twigs and an old fir cone," she went on. "Do you think that will make the soup boil?"

"Wretched twigs and a fir cone!" wailed Logo. "That was Stick Boy. That was my best friend. You've burnt my best friend."

Logo cried so much that he couldn't drink one drop of the soup when it *was* cooked at last, he was so sad.

Everybody was sorry for him, but they all said:

"Fancy crying for a bundle of twigs and a fir cone! What a baby you are!"

Then Logo decided if he ever made another companion he would keep him a secret. "I will make him in a secret place," thought Logo, "and I'll only play with him in the secret place. I'll never show him to anyone else or take him into the village. Then he'll be safe."

It was not very easy to find a secret place. Though the forest was wild and dark, his father and brothers hunted there, and he was not allowed to go far by himself. Besides, he might easily be eaten by a lion or a hyena. There were secret places by the river, among the rushes, but his sisters went there to fetch water, and he might easily be eaten by a crocodile, or stolen away by a snake.

The only secret place he knew was a cave among some rocks, from which a little stream trickled. There was not enough water for the girls to fill their calabashes. Indeed, it was not the sort of place that older people bothered about as it was wet and dark and uncomfortable. But it was just right for a small boy who wanted to be by himself.

As Logo was getting near the door of this secret cave, his foot trod in something sticky and damp. It was a kind of mud, but firmer and more clinging than the mud in the village. He picked up a bit in his hand and rolled it into a ball. It was clay, though he did not know the word. It made a hard, round, pale ball.

Then Logo had an idea. If he could make a ball of this sticky stuff he could make a head, and a body, and arms and legs. He could make a Mud Boy to play with. It took him all day, till the sun went down, to make the Mud Boy. At first he used the clay too wet and it stuck to his hands and to the flat rock he was using as a table. Then he used it too dry and the head kept breaking off the body, and the arms and legs fell off. Then, at last, he used it not too wet and not too dry and he made a nice little Mud Boy with tiny pebbles for eyes and nose and mouth, and fluffy cotton from the tufted cotton grass for his hair.

Logo left him inside the cave on a rocky shelf and hurried home, just in time to hold out his coconut shell for his helping of soup.

The next day the Mud Boy was drier and harder, and Logo brought him into the sun to get drier still. While Logo dozed, the Mud Boy baked in the hot sun and when Logo picked him up he was almost too hot to touch.

"I'll cool you in the waterfall," said Logo, going to a place inside the cave where the water tumbled down the side of a rock. As he held the Mud Boy under the waterfall, something so surprising happened that he almost dropped him. The Mud Boy began to move his arms and legs and turn his head from side to side. Logo quickly put him down on a dry stone.

"Are you alive?" he gasped.

"Yes," said the Mud Boy. "I am. What can I do for you?"

"Could you—could you be my friend?"

"I am your friend," answered the Mud Boy. "I'm your friend for as long as you need me. How can I help you?"

Then Logo explained how lonely he was because he was the youngest and the smallest in the family, and could not do important work like his big brothers and sisters.

"I want to be useful," he said. "I don't like it when people keep saying: 'Get out of the way! Let me do my work in peace! Go and play!' "

"I can teach you many useful things," said the Mud Boy. "You can be more useful to your family than all your brothers and sisters put together. What worries your mother more than anything else?"

Logo thought for a while. "She worries when the soup spills or the monkeys steal the calabashes for carrying the water. But of course the worst thing of all is when the fire goes out."

"Why does it go out?" asked the Mud Boy.

"If there is a terrible thunderstorm and the rain is so heavy that the fire spits and hisses and dies. Then the women weep and wail and the men sit in silence and cover their faces. The strongest and swiftest of the men goes to look for some other tribe living in the forest, perhaps many days' journey away, and perhaps this other tribe has a fire and will give the man a burning stick. And he gives them a gift and hopes to bring the flame safely back so he can light another fire."

"But sometimes the fire stick goes out or he sleeps and

it burns away, then he must go again and take another gift. Till we have a new fire there is no hot soup, and the old people cannot warm themselves and there is nothing to scare off the hungry lion when he comes prowling in the night."

"Tomorrow I will show you the secret of fire," said the Mud Boy. "Bring me a small, half-rotten log and a strong, straight stick."

The next morning Logo went to the cave carrying the log under one arm and the stick in his hand. The Mud Boy lay where he had left him, silent and still.

"Here I am!" said Logo loudly. "Here I am with the things you asked for, the log and the stick."

The Mud Boy took no notice. Logo shook him gently, but he stayed silent and still. Then Logo remembered that the day before he had come to life when held under the waterfall. Perhaps it would be a good thing to try again. He lifted the Mud Boy and held him in the clear, cool ribbon of water. At once he began to twist and turn and shake the drops of water out of his eyes and tufted hair.

"That was good!" he said cheerfully. "Now we can set to work. Make a hole in the rotten part of the log just big enough for the stick to fit in." Logo hollowed out a hole and drove the stick in as far as it would go.

"Now twirl the stick between your hands," said the Mud Boy. "Twirl it between your palms. That's the way. Now just go on and on and on."

The Mud Boy closed his eyes and seemed half asleep while Logo twirled and twirled the stick. Soon his arms ached and he twirled slower and slower.

"Faster! Faster!" urged the Mud Boy, waking up. "Faster! Faster!"

Logo twirled and twirled till his palms were sore and the pain was almost more than he could bear.

"Faster! Faster!" urged the Mud Boy, waking up again. "Faster! Faster!"

"My head aches," sighed Logo. "I ache all over. I'm sick and dizzy. May I drink from the waterfall and cool my burning hands?"

"No! No!" said the Mud Boy. "You must go on. The secret is almost yours. Can't you smell the smell of fire?"

Logo sniffed. Yes, he could smell a scorching smell. He would go on a little longer. His head was spinning round as he twirled and twirled and the face of the Mud Boy sometimes seemed small and far away, and sometimes large and rather frightening. Suddenly there was a spurt of flame and the end of the stick was burning. The secret was his. He had made fire, something no one else in the village had ever done. They only knew the fire that came from the sky when the lightning blasted a tree.

"May I show my family?" asked Logo. "Will the magic work again when I get home?"

"Wait till the fire goes out," said the Mud Boy. "I think you won't have to wait long."

There was a distant rumble of thunder and Logo noticed that what he had taken to be twilight falling was really huge black storm clouds gathering, edged with purple and orange.

"We will go into the cave and keep dry," said the Mud Boy. "Bring the log and stick as well. You mustn't allow them to get damp. Sit with me in the far corner, under this overhanging rock. We shall be all right here."

A moment later there was a flash of lightning and a crash of thunder and the rain fell like a sheet of water.

If Logo had been at home he would have crouched in the hut with the rest of the family, shaking with fear and covering his ears with his hands. But here, in the cave, he felt safe. The Mud Boy did not cover his ears with his hands or close his eyes. He watched as the lightning flashed, and Logo watched as well.

"We are safe and dry," said the Mud Boy. "We are not ants to hide in the ground or monkeys to scream in the tree tops. We can make fire ourselves, if we want. We know the secret."

When the storm was over, the waterfall was twice its size and the stream roared along like a river. Logo took his dry log and stick and splashed his way back to the village. Before he reached the circle of huts he heard the weeping and wailing of the women and the dull thumps as the men beat their chests with their fists. The fire had been put out by the rain and the lightning had not struck a nearby tree to give them new fire.

"Don't cry, mother," said Logo, rubbing his cheek against her wet one. "Don't cry. I can make a new fire."

"Be quiet, my son," said his father. "The gods are angry enough. They have put out the fire we have kept burning for many moons. Do not anger them still more with your idle boasting."

"But I can make a new fire. I can!" whispered Logo. "Watch me carefully."

He sat down on a dry strip of tiger skin and began to twirl his stick in the log. This time he did not mind his aching arms and his sore hands. He knew he would succeed in the end. At first the family watched without much interest, thinking Logo was wasting their time as well as his own. But when they could smell the faint smell of scorching they sat up on their heels and watched intently. He could see his mother clasping her hands together, and his father leaning forward to get a closer view. When the

flame burst out of the hole a shout of joy and wonder went up. The families from the other huts were called and soon the whole tribe came to watch Logo making fire.

It was not easy to get the big fire going as everything was soaking wet, but many of the women kept little hoards of dry twigs and cones in their huts and they gladly brought them out.

Soon the fire leapt and crackled and a great pot of soup was put on to cook. While it cooked, the whole tribe danced round and round, stamping their feet and clapping their hands, and chanting:

Let us praise Logo,
The fire-tender,
The fire-mender,
The fire-maker,
The fire-waker,
The wise and the wonderful.
Let us praise Logo.

After the hot soup everyone went to bed and Logo found, for once, there was plenty of room for him in the hut. He did not have to curl up like a ball. He could stretch out and even turn over. Everyone moved up to give him all the space he needed.

The next morning the old grandfather measured him against the tree trunk and he had grown the width of a thumb. His father made him a bow and arrow and took him out hunting and he shot a lizard and made a skin bag for his mother.

The next day his brothers took him out to herd the cattle and they gave him a new-born calf for his own.

The next day his sisters took him down to the river and let him carry a calabash of water on his head. When it spilt, they only laughed and told him to try again.

The next day his grandfather showed him how to make a pipe from a hollow reed and blow into it so that it made music.

The next day he gathered all the sweet-smelling flowers he could find for his grandmother, because she was blind and this was her only way of enjoying the flowers that grew in the forest.

Logo was now so busy that it was many days before he remembered the Mud Boy in the secret cave. He took his bow and arrow, and his pipe, to show the Mud Boy how big he was growing and how important he was. But when he got to the cave the Mud Boy was not there.

Logo looked everywhere and called him again and again:

"Are you there? Are you there? Are you there?"

His voice echoed in the hollow cave. Faint and far, he thought he heard the Mud Boy saying:

"I am your friend as long as you need me."

Then Logo remembered that his father had promised to take him to gather honey from the nest of the wild bees and that he must hurry. He had so much to do and to learn that he hardly had time for a special friend, even the Mud Boy. He would have to come back another day.

"Goodby!" he called. "Goodby!"

"Goodby!" came the echo, "Goodby!"

Lucky Angus

The young man, Angus, lived in the north on the island of Scale. It was a long day's voyage from the island to the mainland, and the islanders only crossed two or three times a year to do their shopping. There were no shops on Scale, but enough corn was grown for flour, and the few black and white cows gave milk and butter and cheese. The wool of the nimble sheep provided clothes, and speckled hens pecked and clucked round the low doorways of the huts.

Most of the huts were no bigger than a small tent, though families of six or seven or more managed to squeeze inside. But Angus had plenty of room because he lived quite alone. His father and mother were both drowned when their boat overturned in a sudden storm.

There were many girls on the island who would gladly have taken him for a husband as he was a tall, well set-up lad, but he took no more notice of one than the other. He was pleasant and friendly with all.

When the island people visited the mainland for the great spring fair, there was hardly a young girl who did not buy a ribbon or a string of beads for the purpose of attracting Angus's attention. But he only called out cheerfully:

"That's a fine ribbon, Maggie," or "What pretty beads, Janet," and went on his way.

In the summer evenings, when the girls were spinning or knitting, and the boys were running races or mending their nets, Angus set to work to build himself a stone house. There was no stone building on the island except the ruins of an old church; the ordinary huts were simply made of turf with the roofs weighted down with pieces of rock. Angus brought the stones from a quarry among the hills and carried them down to the shore in strong panniers slung on either side of his gray donkey. He laid the stones on top of each other as we make a dry stone wall.

It was many evenings before the stone house was finished. There was a stable beside it for the donkey, who shared it at night with the hens. And there was a turf shed for Angus's tools and fishing nets and anything else which would have made a clutter in the new house.

When the winter set in, Angus was perfectly at home. He kept a good fire of peat and driftwood in the evening and lit the candles in their brass candlesticks and was snug and contented. Only now and then, when he darned his thick, fisherman's socks, he wished there was a brisk young girl on the other side of the hearth who would take the needle (which *would* come unthreaded) out of his hand and fill up the great holes with a lattice of neat strands. He found darning much worse than digging or milking the cows, or even managing a boat in a choppy sea.

Angus was a fisherman in his spare time. When his small fields were sown and the animals fed and cared for, he went out in his boat to catch a fish supper. He could always sell any extra fish to families with more mouths to feed.

One warm spring night, as he drew in his net by the light of the moon, he saw a dark object at the edge of the net, like a bunch of black seaweed. He put out his hand to free the net but drew it back at once. Instead of slippery wet seaweed, he had grasped locks of dripping hair. A face appeared for a moment, white and pointed with great gray eyes, and then there was a gentle splash and the face and the hair vanished. He spent hours casting his net in the same patch of water, but he saw nothing except the moonlight on the ripples.

After this night, Angus lived in a dream. Whatever he was doing, he thought only of the strange face. Wherever he looked, he saw the great gray eyes. He scrambled through his day's work somehow and every evening, when he had had his supper of broth and bread, he went for a walk on the shore. There were no footprints in the sand except his own because the island people were up with the sun and so went to bed early. Once or twice he saw a dark blob among the waves, but he knew it was only a seal swimming in shallow water. There were many seals around the island and the folk could get a high price for their skins, but anyone who killed a seal was visited by such bad luck that seal-hunting was almost unknown.

One evening, Angus walked further than usual and rounded a rocky headland into a little, sheltered cove. There was a flat black rock, bearded with seaweed, in the cove, like a huge flat table, and on this rock sat a group of people. Angus knew at once that they were Selkies, or Seal People, who sometimes came on shore in human form. Sure enough, on the sand beside the rock, he saw their sealskins neatly rolled up.

Angus tingled with excitement. He knew that few people ever saw this rare sight. The Selkies, both men and women, were talking and laughing together, their bodies white in the dusk. Then they sang and their voices blended with the thunder of the waves.

Angus began to creep slowly forward on hands and knees towards the neatly rolled skins, hoping to grab one

and so gain power over the Selkie to whom it belonged. He was almost near enough, when a seagull gave a harsh, warning cry. At once the Selkies leapt to their feet, seized their skins and slipped into them quicker than a hand into a glove, and dived into the water. But quick though they were, Angus reached out and snatched the nearest skin and stuffed it inside his coat.

He saw a pale Selkie with streaming black hair searching in the sand. Then, with a moan of sorrow, she dived into the water after her fellows.

Angus hurried home, following the same line of footprints he had made before. When he was indoors, he lit the candles and took the skin from inside his coat. It was wonderfully soft and fine, more like silk than fur. It was large enough to fit a full-grown woman, yet he could hold it between his two hands as if it were a baby's wrap. He laid it against his cheek and it felt warm, as if someone had just taken it off. When he went to bed, he hid it under his pillow for safety and fell asleep with one hand buried in its softness.

In the middle of the night, Angus opened his eyes and stared into the darkness. A sound had wakened him. At first he thought it was the patter of heavy raindrops on the door of his house. Then he heard the wind whistling in the chimney. But could it be the wind? Did the wind ever sob and sigh like someone whose heart was broken? There was nothing for it but to get out of bed and see for himself.

He left his warm bed and lit the candle and opened the door. A gust of wind and rain came in, and with it a slender, dripping girl, whose black hair hung in dark strands to her waist.

Angus took her cold hand and drew her into the room. Her teeth were chattering and she was shivering from head to foot. He wrapped her in a thick blanket and

gently pushed her into a chair and set light to the fire. He recognized the pale, pointed face and the great gray eyes, though they were now brimming with tears.

"Give me my skin!" begged the Selkie. "Give me my skin."

"No, I cannot do that," said Angus, rubbing her cold hands between his strong, warm ones.

"But I must have my skin. How can I go back to my

own Seal People without my skin?"

"But I don't want you to go back, ever," said Angus. "I want you to marry me and live with me always. I'll love you and work for you and we shall be happy together in this safe stone house."

"My home is under the waves," sighed the Selkie. "This place is like a prison to me. I must go back where I belong. Give me my skin."

"Never," replied Angus. "Never, never, never."

She held out her hands, pleading with him, but he only kissed them and told her again and again that he loved her and that she must be his wife. Suddenly she dried her tears and brushed the wet hair from her face.

"Very well. You are stronger than I am. I will be your wife. But I do not understand the ways of human beings. How can I cook your food and sew for you and keep house when I do not know what to do? Who will teach me?"

"There is a wise old woman on the island named Tabitha and she will teach you. Then, when you have learned the skills of women, you shall come back to me and we will be happy together. What is your name?"

"I cannot tell you," said the Selkie, shaking her head. "Give me a new name to fit my new life. I must forget my old name and my old life."

"I will call you Coral," said Angus.

Coral lived for a while with the wise old Tabitha who taught her to keep house. She learned her lessons well and could soon spin and knit and bake and clean as well as any housewife on the island. The only thing she could not learn was sewing. She pricked her thin fingers till they bled and when Angus saw the blood he snatched the work away and said:

"You shall never shed blood for my sake. I will mend and you can do all the other jobs in the house."

When their wedding day drew near, Tabitha and the other island women made Coral a wedding dress and a veil. She seemed happy enough, but on the evening before her wedding she went for a walk alone along the shore. Angus begged to come with her but she asked him to leave her, saying:

"You will have all the rest of my life. Do you grudge me one hour to myself?"

When Coral came back an hour later, her black hair was wet as if she had been swimming and in her hand she carried a strange and beautiful wedding veil. It was made of net as fine as cobweb and hung from a wreath of shells and sea-flowers. No one had ever seen anything like it before. The only thing that was unpleasant was that it felt cold and slightly damp to the touch.

"Where did it come from? How did you make it? Tell us, do!" said the island women, but Coral only answered:

"It was my mother's wedding veil. It is the kind that my people wear in the place where I come from."

After the wedding day, Coral settled down and seemed content. She kept the stone house clean and when Angus came home in the evening, there was always a good meal on the table, set on a white cloth. It was true that she never again tried to sew, but Angus no longer minded sewing on his own buttons and darning his thick, fisherman's socks, because Coral sang to him and told him stories of ships and whales and storms.

It was well known that a Selkie who lives on the land will always go back to the sea if she can get hold of her sealskin. Angus did not want to take any risks, and he hid Coral's skin in a box and buried the box ten paces from the back door.

When a fine son was born, Angus and Coral were happier than ever before. They laid him in the carved, wooden cradle which had belonged to Angus when he was a baby, and no mother could have loved her child more tenderly. She carried him in her arms up and down the shore, wrapped in a fleecy shawl she had knitted herself from the wool off Angus's sheep. Sometimes a huge black seal swam along beside them, his head turned

towards the land and his eyes fixed on them. Coral held her little son up so that he could see him, and when the child grew older he waved his hand and laughed.

On their wedding day, when they had been married a year, Coral said to her husband:

"Will you grant me just one wish?"

"I will grant every wish, if I can," replied Angus.

"Then just today, as it is our wedding day, let me hold my sealskin in my hands again. After all, it *is* mine."

Angus looked troubled.

"How do I know that you will not slip into it, quick as a

fish jumping, and go back to the sea?"

Coral looked at the cradle and rocked it gently and said:

"While there is a baby in the cradle, I promise that I will never leave you."

So Angus went away and dug up the box and took out the skin and handed it to his wife. She danced for joy and held it against her cheek and kissed it and stroked it. Then she shook it free from dust and brushed it and aired it in the sun. All day she kept touching it and when the sun set, she rolled it up into a neat bundle and gave it to her husband with tears in her eyes, but without speaking a word.

This time he hid the box behind a loose stone in the chimney and for another year neither of them spoke of the skin.

When the second wedding day came round, the first child was crawling on all fours like a fat puppy and could walk a few steps. And in the cradle was a new baby, dark and pale like his brother and beautiful as a dream. So Angus once more took the box from its hiding place in the chimney and let his wife have her sealskin for a day. Once again she danced for joy and held it against her cheek and kissed it and stroked it, and when the sun set she gave it up without a word. This time Angus hid it in

the middle of a sack of wool.

As the years went by, their family of fine children increased till there were seven of them, five boys as dark and pale as their mother, and two girls as fair and rosy as their father. There was room for them all in the stone house and the other islanders declared they had never seen such beautiful children or such a good mother.

When the children were only babies, Coral took them down to the shore and undressed them and held them in a pool at the foot of the flat Table Rock. Angus was shocked at first and feared that they would come to some harm, but when he saw the little things kicking their tiny legs and flapping their little brown arms, chuckling with joy, he knew that all was well. Indeed, each child learned to swim as easily as to walk and the mother and children frisked and splashed together like a family of dolphins.

Angus had seven years of good luck. His cows bore strong calves and gave rich milk. His hens laid fine brown eggs. His few sheep never strayed away into the hills. When food was scarce, he had only to put out to sea in his boat and cast his net, and it was full in no time. He became known everywhere as Lucky Angus.

As the children were born, Angus wanted Coral to choose their names.

"Why not choose a name from your old life?" he said, hoping to please her. But she shook her head and said that she did not wish to let the language of the Selkies pass her lips again. So together they chose names which seemed suitable to them, though strange to the island folk. The two girls were named Mist and Sea Pink and the five boys were named after objects on the shore or in the sea.

When the eighth child was born, Angus's luck left him.

It was another boy, dark and pale like his brothers, but very small and feeble. He was always crying and would not feed or sleep. However tenderly Coral rocked the cradle or hushed him in her arms, nothing would soothe him. After a few days he died and was buried in the graveyard beside the ruined church. The island folk laid what flowers they could gather on the grave, and Coral brought shells and wreaths of seaweed.

The other seven children soon forgot the little brother who had stayed with them for such a short time, and Angus hoped his wife would soon forget too. He put the cradle up in the loft so that it would not remind her of her baby as she went about her work.

The next time their wedding day came round, Coral asked, as before, to see her sealskin and Angus took it from its hiding place, which had been changed so many times and was now inside an old fisherman's jersey, hanging in the shed.

She did not dance and clap her hands as she used to, but she shook it and brushed it and examined every inch several times to make sure that no moth had settled there, and no mouse had left its tooth marks. When she was satisfied that it was in good condition, without stain or blemish, she hung it on the sunny window-sill to air.

Suddenly she pointed out of the window and caught

her husband by the arm and cried out:

"Look, Angus! Up on the hill! The black dog is among the sheep. He has chased them out of sight!"

Angus picked up a stout stick and ran off up the hill, as this black dog had worried many sheep on the island and killed two lambs. His four eldest children, small though they were, ran panting after him.

Coral was left with the two youngest boys who were sitting on the doorstep, playing with pebbles and a bowl of water. The youngest girl, Sea Pink, was at her side, fingering her belt which she had decorated with flat shells.

Coral snatched her sealskin, rolled it up and tucked it under her arm. She took the little girl by the hand and they went together towards the shore. Coral took such long strides that the child had to run to keep up. When they came to the Table Rock, Coral kissed Sea Pink and gave her the pearl necklace from her own neck which Angus had given her as a wedding present.

"I shall have all the pearls in the wide ocean," Coral said, seeing the child's surprised face. Then she took off her clothes, folded them neatly, and slipped into her sealskin as a hand slips into a glove. As she dived into the water, a great black seal came swimming towards her and they both disappeared under the waves.

Angus searched the hills far and wide for hours, but found his flock feeding peacefully and no sign of the killer dog. When he got home, he saw the two little boys still playing on the doorstep, but he could not see his wife or Sea Pink. He looked on the window-sill where the seal-skin had been airing and saw that it was not there. Then he remembered the empty cradle in the loft and ran off as fast as he could to the shore. He followed his wife's firm, narrow footprints and the marks of the child's bare feet. When he came to Table Rock and saw the neat pile of clothes and his daughter playing with the pearl necklace, he knew what had happened.

"Where is mother? Where has she gone?" he asked again and again, but the little one was too young to talk much. She could only point to the sea and say:

"Mother gone," and hold up the beads and say:

"Mother's pretty beads."

It was a sad, silent man who cooked the children's supper and washed them and put them to bed.

The next morning, though he had barred the door the night before, he found a trail of wet prints across the floor and on the children's blankets were traces of seaweed and a few tiny shells. Their pillows felt damp to touch, though he could only guess whether they were wet from salt water or salt tears.

The following morning there were the same signs of a visitor and so, on the third night, he did not go to bed, but sat in a chair in the corner of the room, in the shadows, and watched. Soon after midnight he heard the faint sound of bare feet and someone sighed softly. The light of the moon came through the window and he saw his wife, her sealskin flung round her like a cloak, going from cradle to cot, and from bed to bed, laying her cheek on each pillow in turn.

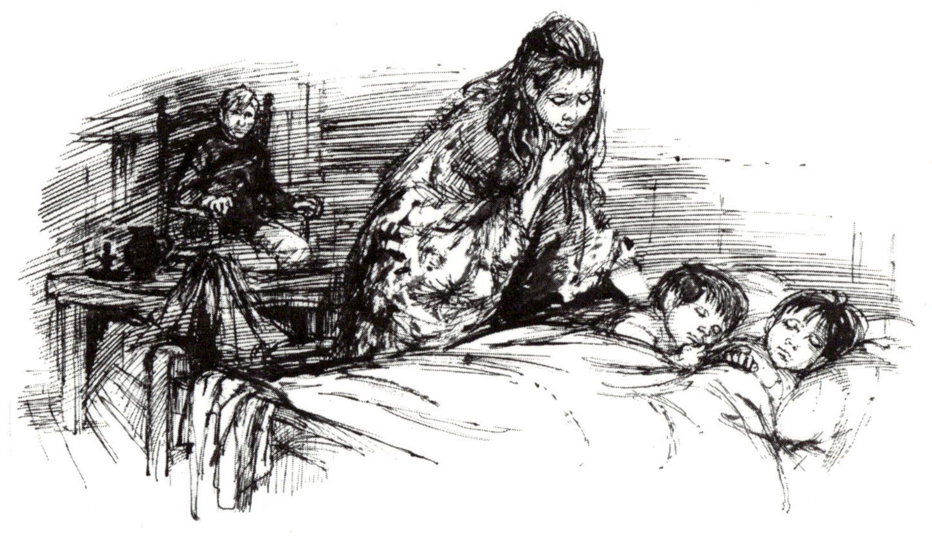

As she walked by the dark corner where he sat, he sprang from his chair and seized her round the waist and called her. She did not try to get free, but followed him into the living-room where he lit the candles.

"Will you never come back?" he pleaded. "How can I care for seven children who need their mother?"

"I will not lie to you, Angus," she replied softly. "I shall never come back. I have seven children in the sea and I must go back to them and live among my own people. But when one of our little ones has a birthday, send the child down to the shore so that I may give my good wishes and some small gift. And on our wedding day, if you still love me, come yourself. Then you can tell me how things are with you. Goodby, and forgive me if you can. I am only doing what I must."

She slipped out into the night, leaving Angus to his own sad thoughts.

Angus remembered Coral's words, and when the children's birthdays came round, he sent them to the shore and Coral rose from the waves and called them by name and gave them a gift from the world under the water. The girls had necklaces of pearl and bracelets of coral and brooches of amber. The boys had little ships and animals carved from the bones of fishes and toys made from shells.

On their wedding day, Angus himself went down to the shore and Coral rose up and called him by name. He told her all that had happened in the last year, both the doings of the children and the happenings on the farm.

He was still called "Lucky Angus" by the island folk

because he had only to cast his net into the water and at once it was full of fish. But he himself believed that his luck had left him for ever the day Coral put on her seal-skin and went back to the Selkies.

A Winter's Tale

In the middle of the night, Dirk woke up. He opened his eyes and stared into the darkness. He could hear his father and mother breathing in their big bed in the opposite corner of the hut. The only light came from the log on the dying fire which glowed a dull red. The log made a slight noise as it settled in the hearth.

Something had waked him, he was sure. What could it be? He never woke up till it was morning, when his mother blew the fire and his father went outside to milk the goats.

He slipped out of his little bed and tiptoed across the cold stone floor to the window. Outside the stars were bright, though he could not see each separate twinkling light because the window was iced over. He breathed on a piece of window pane to soften the ice and then rubbed himself a peep-hole with his warm fingers. He peered closely through the round of clear glass. A large, soft, dark eye was peering back from outside.

Dirk stared and stared, unblinking, and the large, soft, dark eye stared back at him.

He suddenly longed to be in his bed again, with the blankets huddled round his shoulders and his face buried in the goose-feather pillow. He turned and ran from the window, too quickly to feel the cold of the flagstones, and scrambled into bed.

"I shall never, never get to sleep again," he thought. "I may have to go into Mother's bed as I did when I was little and had a bad dream. Is there a traveler out there, his cloak freezing to his shoulders? But a traveler would knock on the door and my father would hear and let him in. Or is there a robber out in the cold and darkness? In the morning I shall look in the snow for the prints of his boots. Or is it a ghost, the ghost of some poor man lost in the snow? His feet would leave no prints."

But while Dirk was puzzling and wondering, he fell into a deep sleep and did not stir till he heard his mother blowing the fire with the leather bellows.

"Mother!" he called out. "I woke in the night and went to the window and saw someone looking in. At least I saw his big dark eye. Then I was frightened and went back to bed."

Just then his father came in with the bowl of goat's milk for breakfast.

"You had a dream, my son," he said knocking the snow off his boots with a stick.

"No! No! No! I remember everything exactly. The log was still glowing a little and you and Mother were asleep. I rubbed myself a peep-hole on the window. Look, and you will see it for yourself!"

But the peep-hole had iced over like the rest of the window.

"Dreams are strange things," said his mother. "I've often dreamed I was at the market, plain as daylight, with my basket of cheeses beside me. But I've waked up and found myself warm and safe in bed, praise be!"

"I know it wasn't a dream because it didn't feel like a dream. I shall look for footmarks in the snow when I go out to play."

"Listen, Dirk," went on his father. "I think you really did get out of bed and go to the window. But the eye you saw was a reflection of your own eye, like looking in a mirror. There was no stranger outside, staring in. That isn't possible."

After breakfast, Dirk opened the top drawer in the chest and took out one of his dearest treasures. It was a box, lined with velvet, with sea-shells stuck on the lid. But he was not interested in the velvet lining or the shells just then. He was interested in the circle of looking glass inside the lid. He gazed into this tiny mirror, putting his face close so that he could only see one dark eye with its fringe of long eyelashes and curved eyebrows above. The eye was round. The strange eye that had stared at him from outside was larger and more oval. His father was wrong.

When he had put on his thick coat and hood, and gone out to play, he looked carefully below the window. The snow was marked with little pits, which might have been the hoof marks of the goats or even of his father's stick. But snow had slid off the roof and partly covered the marks. He saw nothing which might have been the prints of a robber's feet, shod in great black boots with fur round the top.

The next night Dirk woke up again, long before morning. The log was glowing faintly and he could hear his father and mother breathing. Something had waked him up. What could it be? He lay and listened, his eyes wide open.

Then he heard a sharp tap-tap, like someone rapping on the window. Tap-tap-tap, then a pause. Then tap-tap-tap, again. He got out of bed and crossed the cold stone floor. He breathed on the window and rubbed with his whole hand till he had cleared a wider space than before.

The tapping started again and he saw something like a forked branch. Yet it wasn't an ordinary branch with twigs at the side. It was a thick, hard thing. It reminded him of something but he couldn't remember what.

Then the tapping stopped and there was a scurry of

feet and a soft thud as the visitor made off.

Dirk looked at his sleeping parents. His father's mouth was not quite shut and he was gently snoring. It was useless to wake him. He would be angry. He would order Dirk back to bed. His mother would be displeased, too. And he dared not try to open the heavy door himself, clanking the iron chain and grating the key in the lock. They would both wake. He must go back to bed.

As he buried his face in the pillow, thinking of travelers, robbers and ghosts, he knew that if he could only remember what that branched stick reminded him of, he could solve the mystery. But he went on thinking of ghosts. They were white. (But this one was dark.) They were silent. (But this one made a noise with its feet. It thumped the snow.) They should be treated gently and comforted. (But this one was locked out in the cold.)

While he was wondering about ghosts, sleep overtook him and the next thing he knew was that morning had come and his mother was lighting the fire and singing softly to herself.

During breakfast, Dirk laid down his spoon and said: "Something tapped on the window in the night. I heard it. And I saw it."

"You were dreaming, my son. There is no tree near enough to the hut for its branches to tap on the pane. And no bird would be on the wing in the darkness, to tap with its beak."

"But father, I heard it. And saw it. I saw something dark like a branch. But it wasn't a branch."

"You had too much supper, perhaps," said his mother, teasing him. "Now if you had had just a slice of dry bread instead of broth——"

Then she saw by Dirk's face that his feelings were hurt. No one would believe him. His lips were trembling. He bent his head over his wooden bowl to hide his tears. She quickly put an arm round his shoulders.

"Dreams can be as clear as daylight," she said softly. "Don't be upset. Perhaps there was a sharp shower of hail in the night, knocking on the window. Who knows? Shall I move your bed beside mine tonight? Would that be better?"

"No thank you, mother. I am not a baby any longer. And it wasn't the broth. Or the hail. It was real."

When he went out to play, Dirk was still unsettled and unhappy. He wanted to run a long way very fast. He wanted to chop down a tree or saw a huge log. He wanted to show that he was strong and sensible, not a silly little child who mixed up dreams with real things.

He took his sled from inside the goats' shed and pulled it after him up the hill towards the birch forest. Then, later, he could coast down the hill back to the hut.

As he ran, dragging the sled behind him, he began to cheer up. His feet and fingers glowed with warmth. His cheeks were red as holly berries. Even his lips tingled. He would have sung for joy if he had had any breath to spare.

Before the forest began, there was a cluster of birch trees by themselves, around a little pond. The pond was frozen over now and he liked to slide on it. He dropped the rope of his sled and ran to the edge. But before he set foot on the shining ice he stopped short. A brown shape was standing among the trees. When Dirk saw the large, sad, dark eyes and the great branching antlers on the head, he remembered what he had forgotten. The animal was a reindeer.

"It was you," he said softly, "who looked through my window with your dark eye."

"Yes," said the reindeer, "it was."

"And it was you who tapped on the window pane with your antler."

"Yes, it was."

"I would have let you in if I could. Truly I would. But my father and mother thought I was dreaming."

"Fathers and mothers don't know everything," said the reindeer.

"But they know a lot," said Dirk. "What did you want? Why did you knock?"

"I wanted a friend," said the reindeer. "I am alone, just as you are alone. It is good to have a friend."

"I should like to be friends," said Dirk. "Perhaps my father would let you sleep in the warm shed with the goats. They are nice goats, and every spring the nanny goat has a kid. And my mother would feed you. Perhaps she would braid you a halter."

The reindeer became restless when he heard this and stamped his hoofs and swung his head from side to side. He prodded the frozen snow with his antlers.

"No, thank you. I do not ask for a prison."

"But I said 'shed', not 'prison'."

"Shed, hut, prison, they are all the same to me. Four walls and a roof and a door that is locked and bolted from the outside."

"My father would only lock it to keep the wolf out and to keep you safe."

"What care I for the wolf? I can keep myself safe. No, thank you. Keep your prison. Keep your halter as you call it. If we are friends, we must be friends in the open air, not within walls. We must both come and go as we choose and not be led by a halter."

He trembled with rage and Dirk felt uncomfortable.

If only he could calm him.

"I quite understand," he replied gently. "Of course we will be friends in the open air. I like that best too. There's no room to play in the hut. I will be your friend out here in the snow."

The reindeer stopped trembling and prodding with his antlers. He stood quietly. Dirk put out his hand and touched his new friend. He stroked his rough hair and followed the branching of his antlers with his fingers.

"You are beautiful," he said. "More beautiful than the goats. Where do you live?"

"Away among the mountains," said the reindeer, jerking his head towards the vast, snowy slopes beyond the forest. "Many miles away."

"I must go home," said Dirk. "Dinner will be ready."

"But you will come back?"

"Yes. Tomorrow I will come back."

He got on his sled, kicked off with his heels, and sped down the slope. He was going too fast to look back or he would have seen the reindeer watching him intently till he was out of sight.

As he ate his dinner, Dirk kept thinking of the reindeer's words: "Fathers and mothers don't know everything," and though he meant to tell his father and mother about his new friend, he hardly knew how to begin.

"Father," he said, while his mother turned the brown, spicy pudding out of the basin, "have you ever seen a reindeer in the forest?"

"No," said his father, "but your grandfather once found one. It was a hard winter and the poor thing was only a bag of bones. It was lying by the little pond where you play. Reindeer don't come down as far as this unless they are hunted and there are few hunters this way. It is too wild and lonely."

"What happened to the one grandfather saw?"

"It died. In the spring, when the ground was soft, he buried its bones by the pool."

"Do you think I might see a reindeer one day?"

"No, there's no chance. When you are bigger and we go further north you might see a herd in the mountains."

He would never believe me, thought Dirk. He'd say I was dreaming. I won't tell.

That night there was nothing to disturb him and he slept soundly till morning. After breakfast, he ran outside and took his sled and set off to the birch tree pool. His new friend was there already, stamping his hoofs with impatience. He looked closely at Dirk's face.

"You didn't tell your father and mother about me?"

"No," replied Dirk.

"Good! They wouldn't have believed you. Or if they

had believed, they would be thinking out some plan to keep me safe, to shut me up till the spring, perhaps. Now if you like, I'll pull you along on your sled."

"There isn't enough rope," said Dirk.

"No. There isn't. You'll have to get on my back and have a ride."

Dirk wanted a ride but he felt frightened. The reindeer looked so strong, as though he could run like the wind. He might even run away to the snowy mountains with Dirk clinging to his back. His new friend seemed to read his thoughts.

"I won't gallop," he said. "I'll trot gently. And I'll stop directly you tell me."

So Dirk climbed on to his back and the reindeer set off, gently trotting. Dirk held on to his antlers and felt safe. It was even better than tobogganing. He would have liked to ride on for ever.

When they reached the forest and Dirk had to duck his head to keep out of the way of the branches, he asked the reindeer to turn, which he did at once, bringing Dirk safely back to the pool.

The winter days flew by. Every day Dirk played with the reindeer and had rides on his back, and when he went to bed he slept so deeply that the night seemed like a few minutes.

Sometimes his father or mother asked at breakfast:

"Have you had any dreams, Dirk? Has anyone been tapping on the window?"

And he answered truthfully:

"Never a dream! Morning comes so quickly that I haven't time to dream."

But he never told them about his morning rides.

The reindeer began to go faster and further, and though he always turned back when Dirk asked him, he seemed sorry to turn. He liked going on and on.

One day there was a high wind which had an edge like a knife. Dirk's mother wanted him to stay indoors, but he laughed and put on his thickest clothes and wound a red muffler twice round his neck. Even then, the bitter wind seemed to pierce to his bones. He found the reindeer stamping his hoofs and leaping in the air to keep warm.

"This is my kind of weather," he said cheerfully. "This wind comes straight from the snowy mountains where I live."

"I think it's too cold for a ride," shivered Dirk.

"Nonsense! Bend low over my neck and bury your cheek in my mane. You'll soon feel warm. Up you get!"

Dirk climbed on to the reindeer's back and crouched down and he certainly felt warmer than on the ground. There was a sharp flurry of snow and he closed his eyes as the flakes whirled in his face. He was very comfortable now and the reindeer ran specially fast. Dirk could hardly hear the thudding hoofs in the snow. He felt as if he were flying. When he peered through his eyelashes and saw the snow he might have been on the back of some wonderful bird, carried with the wind.

The wind made a noise like thunder or a great waterfall. The noise seemed to be inside his head. When he called out: "Please, turn back!" he was not surprised that his friend did not hear and went straight on. His voice sounded as thin and small as a bird's chirping. He called out again, but the words were whirled away with the snowflakes.

Dirk began to feel sleepy. It doesn't matter, he thought drowsily. It doesn't really matter. Perhaps the reindeer has turned back and I don't know it. We shall be home soon.

Half dreaming and half sleeping, they sped on. Dirk did not feel cold or anxious, only sleepy. He murmured, "Home soon! Home soon!" till he was not sure if he were saying the words, or the reindeer, or perhaps the wind.

Suddenly the reindeer stopped sharply. Dirk gripped his mane to stop himself from falling off.

"Here we are," said the reindeer kindly. "Here we are at last."

Dirk rolled off his back on to the ground, expecting to see his own wooden hut, but there was only a dark cave with a lantern burning over the entrance. He staggered inside, stiff from his long, cold ride, and found a fire burning. There were rushes spread on the floor.

"But where am I? I want to go home!" he called out.

"You *are* home," said the reindeer triumphantly. "This is our home. Lie down and sleep."

Dirk wanted to cry. He wanted to shout and be angry. But he was too tired. He lay down on the rushes beside the fire. The last thing he remembered was the reindeer bending over him, lumps of snow between his antlers and

icicles round his mouth and his eyelashes frozen and sparkling. His eyes were dark and sad.

Dirk and the reindeer settled down together to a life which seemed to Dirk like a fairy tale. There was always food to eat, bread and broth and fruit for him, and mosses for the reindeer. The fire was always blazing and the lamp above the doorway burned all night. The reindeer lay near the opening to the cave where it was cold, and Dirk lay by the warm fire. They spent hours and hours talking and although they often disagreed, they never quarreled.

"Take me back to my home," pleaded Dirk one day.

"It is better here," said the reindeer. "Here you can be a boy for ever and have rides on my back, and in the spring you can gather the mountain flowers and play by the flowing streams. If you had stayed in the hut you would have to grow up and milk the goats and cut down trees and work all day long. Here it is always holiday time and you are always young."

After many days, Dirk began to dream at nights as he lay on the rushes. He dreamed of home. He saw his mother blowing the fire with the leather bellows, or turning the brown spicy pudding out of its basin. He saw his father carrying the bowl of goats' milk, or bringing in logs from the wood-pile. Sometimes he heard their gentle breathing in the darkness as if they were sleeping nearby. After these dreams of home, he woke with a feeling of unbearable sadness.

"If you are my friend," he said to the reindeer, "take me back. I think I can hear my mother crying and see my father's face full of longing."

"They do not miss you," said the reindeer. "See I will show you." He set a bowl of water outside the cave and when it had frozen over, he lifted off the circle of ice that covered it. "Look in this mirror," he said.

Dirk looked. At first the ice was cloudy. Then it cleared and he found he was looking right through it into the hut, as if he were looking through the window. He saw his father and mother bending over a cradle. His mother stooped and lifted out a baby wrapped in a shawl. She unfolded the shawl and he saw a tiny, waving hand. His mother kissed the little hand and then folded the shawl back in its place. His father watched and then touched the down on the baby's head with a gentle finger.

"You see?" said the reindeer. "They have a new baby to love. They have forgotten you."

Dirk did not dream that night. He woke with the rushes wet from his tears.

Every day the reindeer went out for a run in the snow. Sometimes Dirk went too. Sometimes he stayed in the cave. One day, when he had stayed behind, he took a bowl of water and set it outside to freeze as the reindeer had done. Then he lifted off the circle of ice and gazed at it.

At first it was cloudy. Then it cleared and he could see right into the hut as before. His mother was gently rocking the cradle with her foot, and his father was making a small bow and arrow.

"Our baby daughter is precious and beautiful," said his mother, "but I cannot be happy without Dirk. It is now three months since he disappeared."

"I think of him day and night," said his father. "Now that I have finished this bow and arrow for him I shall make a fur hat and a fur belt. When he comes home, he will jump for joy."

"When he comes home," repeated his mother. "When will that be?"

Then the ice mirror clouded and Dirk could see no more. But he was no longer sad. His father and mother loved him as much as ever. He must, somehow, get home. While he was trying to think out a plan, he braided some reeds together and made a rope. It kept his fingers occupied while his mind was busy.

When the reindeer came in with snowflakes frozen on his mane, he seemed upset. He jerked his head and stamped and snorted.

"What is it, friend?" asked Dirk.

"It is that—that rope you are making," said the reindeer. "It upsets me. I can't look at it. Please hide it somewhere."

So Dirk hid it under his red muffler and the reindeer settled down peacefully for the evening.

The next morning the reindeer caught sight of the end of the braided reeds and began to tremble.

"Take that thing away!" he said in an angry voice, quite different from his usual gentle tone. "We can't go on being friends with a thing like that in the cave. I shall go out for my run in the snow. Burn that thing while I am gone." He galloped off, much put out.

But Dirk did not burn the reed plait. He added to it as quickly as his fingers could work till he had a long, strong, tough rope. He hid this under a stone by the fire, in a place which was too hot for the reindeer.

When the reindeer came in he was in a good temper again. He glanced round the cave and saw the red muffler hanging up on the wall. There was no sign of the rope. He sighed with relief and was specially kind to Dirk for the rest of the day, telling him stories and allowing him to polish his antlers.

That night, when the reindeer slept, Dirk lay awake. He was too excited to sleep. In the middle of the night he softly took the plait from under the stone and put it twice round the reindeer's neck. It went round easily and there were two long ends to spare. He tied these tightly together to make a loop, like reins.

When the reindeer woke up he felt the rope and gave a great leap into the air. He pawed the ground and twisted his neck and tried to break the hated thing with his antlers, or bite it through with his teeth. But it was too close to his neck. He could not reach it. He rolled his fine dark eyes and Dirk saw a few flecks of foam at the corner of his mouth.

"Take it off!" he begged. "Take this horrible thing off my neck. I will carry you home on my back today—this minute—if you will set me free."

Dirk longed to do what his friend asked, but he did not trust him.

"I will take the rope off when you set me down by my hut," he said firmly. "Not before."

The reindeer fought to get rid of the rope till he was

worn out, only stopping to beg and plead with Dirk to help him. Dirk wanted to help, but he wanted even more to get home. At last the reindeer stopped struggling and said quietly:

"Get on to my back."

Dirk joyfully put on his outdoor clothes and twisted the red muffler round his neck and climbed on to the familiar brown back. He held on to the braided rope and the reindeer galloped off. As before, he ran like the wind and the rush of cold air made Dirk feel sleepy. After many hours the reindeer stopped suddenly, and Dirk slid off his back in front of the door of his hut.

Quickly he unlooped the bridle from the reindeer's neck.

"Thank you, thank you, Dirk," cried the reindeer. "I feared you were going to tie me up in the shed with the goats and make me your slave."

"Oh, I couldn't do that!" answered Dirk, rubbing his cheek against the reindeer's rough one. "You are my best friend. Will you come and see me again?"

"Perhaps. Who knows? Goodby, Dirk," and the reindeer bowed his head and shook his antlers and Dirk waved back as he galloped away.

If the reindeer had looked in his magic mirror he would have seen Dirk hugged and kissed by his father and mother.

Then proudly trying on the new fur hat and belt and twanging the new bow. Then he would have seen him sitting in the wooden rocking-chair, nursing his new baby sister, who laughed and cooed to see her big brother.

RUTH AINSWORTH BEST SELLERS

JACK FROST

". . . four wintry tales, all quite different in theme and as crisp and fresh as the season itself . . . Miss Ainsworth conjures up colourful characters and intriguing situations. The fairy-tale nature of the stories is enhanced by the fact that each of them starts with a familiar scene, wanders off into fantasy, and returns to earth with the greatest ease"—*Times Educational Supplement*

"Four excellent new longish home and magic stories for the very young by one of our most skilled practitioners in this field"—*Naomi Lewis in Trade News*

LOOK, DO AND LISTEN

"Just the thing for any mother or pre-school teacher trying to get a good start in expanding a child's language through simple stories, verse and games. There's a lot of suggested action also to help him develop and enjoy his new physical skills"—*The Guardian*

"This is real treasure trove for youngsters. Old tales, new tales, finger games and nursery rhymes; they are all here in a glorious pot-pourri . . . it will serve parents and teachers very well indeed, to say nothing of the children"—*School Librarian*

"A compilation of inestimable value to the parent who wishes to encourage creative mental participation of her child"—*Vogue*